Getting the Act Together

Provision for Pupils with Special Educational Needs

A Management Handbook for Schools and Local Education Authorities

1992

0118860925

LONDON: HMSO

Applications for reproduction should be made to HMSO
First published November 1992
Second impression April 1993

Printed in the UK for the Audit Commission and HMI at Press-on-Printers
ISBN 011 886092 5

London : HMSO

Preface

This management handbook is a companion volume to the joint report of the Audit Commission and Her Majesty's Inspectorate of Schools (HMI), *Getting in on the Act*, which described provision for pupils with special educational needs in England and Wales. This handbook presents in detail practice which schools and local education authorities (LEAs) should implement in order to provide more effectively for pupils with special needs. This advice is appropriate for all types of state-funded schools – LEA-maintained ordinary schools, grant-maintained schools and special schools – and for LEAs.

Since the publication of the Audit Commission/HMI report, the Government have published a White Paper on education[1]. The good practice described in this handbook applies both to the current educational régime and to the new régime envisaged in the White Paper.

The study was led for the Audit Commission by Paul Vevers from the Local Government Studies Directorate of the Commission and for HMI by Bob Dyke, an Inspector specialising in this area. Martin Cook, seconded to the Audit Commission from Price Waterhouse, was the auditor on the study team.

The Audit Commission and HMI would like to thank all those schools and LEAs which have been willing to discuss openly their experience of different strategies for providing for pupils with special needs. The interpretation of the findings of the study are those of the Audit Commission and HMI alone.

Between the publication of the national report and this handbook, the office of Her Majesty's Chief Inspector of Schools (OHMCI) was established on 1st September 1992. It will be known as the Office for Standards in Education(OFSTED); HMI form its professional staff. The fieldwork for the study predates this change; references to HMI throughout the text should be taken as applying to the position before 1 September 1992.

---

1   *Choice and Diversity. A new framework for schools. Department for Education (DFE) and Welsh Office. 1992.*

Contents

SUMMARY OF POINTS FOR ACTION   1

INTRODUCTION   5

PART ONE:

CHAMPIONS OF CHILDREN WITH SPECIAL NEEDS?

A rôle for LEAs and schools in co-operation   9

— 1. The Special Needs Policy   11

— 2. The Identification of Pupils with Special Educational Needs   17

— 3. Increasing the Capability of Ordinary Schools   23

— 4. Managing the Process of Assessment and Issuing Statements   31

— 5. Delegating Resources to Schools   37

    (i) Resources for Pupils with Special Needs but without Statements   37

    (ii) Resources for Pupils with Statements   42

— 6. The Accountability of Schools and LEA Support Teams   47

    (i) Monitoring Schools' Performance with Pupils with Special Needs   47

    (ii) Monitoring the Performance of LEA Special Needs Support Teams   52

    (iii) The Accountability of Schools for the Resources which they Receive for Pupils with Special Needs   55

    (iv) Evaluation of Classroom Provision   59

— 7. Controlling Special School Costs   63

— 8. Rationalising Special School Provision   69

PART TWO:

IMPROVING THE QUALITY OF LEARNING FOR PUPILS WITH SPECIAL NEEDS

Additional issues for schools and teachers   75

— Preface to Part Two   77

— 9. Improving the Quality of Lessons for Pupils with Special Needs   79

— 10. Managing Extra Adults in the Classroom   83

— 11. Monitoring the Performance of Teachers with Pupils of Lower Ability   87

Summary of Points for Action

Schools and LEAs in England and Wales provide for an estimated 1.2 million pupils with special educational needs, including almost 170,000 who have a formal statement of special needs. The cost of providing for these pupils was an estimated £1.5 billion in 1990/91. The Audit Commission/HMI report, *Getting in on the Act*[1], which described the provision made by schools and LEAs in England and Wales for these pupils, made recommendations for action at national and local levels to improve the effectiveness of this service. This handbook provides detailed guidance for schools and LEAs on the action which should be taken at the local level:

LEAs and schools should adopt a 'client/contractor' relationship

A key recommendation is greater separation of the rôles of LEAs and schools. LEAs should adopt the rôle of client in a client/contractor relationship, and schools as contractors should be given full responsibility for providing for pupils with special educational needs. Resources should be delegated to schools and they should be held accountable for their achievements. This relationship offers LEAs the opportunity to develop a rôle as champions of children with special educational needs.

LEAs and schools should publish and monitor special needs policies

The starting point for LEAs and schools is to set out their special needs policies. Although many LEAs and schools have produced special needs policies, not all monitor their implementation with objective measures. Monitoring enables them to assess the impact of policy (Section 1).

Schools and LEAs should establish systems to identify consistently pupils with special needs

Once the policy has been determined, the first task is for schools and the LEA to identify consistently children whose special needs should trigger the provision of extra help. LEAs and schools should implement the proposed guidance from the Department for Education (DFE) and Welsh Office[2] on the criteria to be taken into account when determining which children should be assessed and for which children LEAs should issue statements. LEAs, in co-operation with schools, should draw up guidelines to enable schools to identify more consistently pupils with special needs which may not be severe enough to trigger formal assessments (Section 2).

---

1   *Getting in on the Act. Provision for Pupils with Special Needs: the National Picture. HMSO. 1992.*

2   *Special Educational Needs – Access to the System. A Consultation Paper. DFE. 1992. Welsh Office. 1992.*

LEAs should work with schools to improve schools' capability in meeting special needs

Having identified pupils' needs, ordinary schools are required to use their best endeavours to meet them. Schools vary considerably in their capability in meeting special needs and LEAs have a rôle in increasing that capability. This is an essential step in managing the demand for statements, as these should be issued only when ordinary schools cannot provide effectively for a child. Increasing schools' capability should reduce the need for statements. LEAs should use their advice and specialist resources to increase the skills and facilities of ordinary schools in providing for pupils with special needs (Section 3).

Statements should be issued in a timely manner

If it has been decided that a child needs help which ordinary schools cannot provide, the LEA should assess the child and decide quickly whether a formal statement is required and, if so, issue it speedily. Delay in this process is the main complaint of parents of pupils with special needs. The best performing LEAs show that with the use of individual targets and close monitoring of performance by managers, the process can be completed in a reasonable time (Section 4).

LEAs should consider delegating funds for pupils with special needs without statements to ordinary schools according to the actual incidence of those pupils

Distributing funds to schools for pupils with special needs but without statements is a problem for many LEAs. The delegation of funds is sometimes inconsistent because of inaccurate information on the number of pupils with special needs in each school. It is quite practical for LEAs to develop systems which record the actual incidence of pupils with special needs in each school and use these as the basis for the distribution of funds for pupils with special needs without statements (Section 5).

Schemes for determining the funds delegated to schools for pupils with statements should enable funds to be targeted accurately according to pupils' needs

Difficulties in assessing the level of funding for schools also arise in respect of pupils with statements. Some LEAs have delegated funds to schools for these pupils by classifying them into a few broad categories and allocating a sum of money accordingly. Schools may receive the same amount of money for pupils with quite different levels of need but who fall within the same funding band. This is less of a problem where pupils are placed in groups in special units in ordinary schools, where over-funding of some pupils may be counterbalanced by under-funding of others. Where pupils with statements are placed in ordinary classes, LEAs should consider schemes which provide for the amount of funds to be determined individually on the basis of published rules and principles (Section 5).

Schools and LEA special needs support teams should be accountable for their performance with pupils with special needs

Accountability should go hand-in-hand with the delegation of funds to schools. Schools should be held responsible for the use of resources and for what they have achieved with them. Objective indicators of schools' performance in this area can be an incentive to schools to achieve

2

well. But it is not only schools which support pupils with special needs. LEAs should monitor the performance of their special needs support teams (Section 6).

Inspection of schools' special needs provision should focus on its impact on individual pupils

Inspection of practice in the classroom is another important part of accountability. Effective inspection involves focusing on the impact of teaching practice on individual pupils with special needs (Section 6).

LEAs should reallocate special needs resources in line with changes in the pupil population

LEAs must also be accountable for their stewardship of special needs funds. Many of them need to take action to reallocate staff and other resources in line with the trend for an increasing proportion of pupils to be educated in ordinary rather than special schools (Section 7).

LEAs should review their special schools and rationalise them where appropriate

Releasing staffing resources is only one of a number of issues in the special school sector. Teaching the full range of subjects under the National Curriculum is a problem for small special schools with limited numbers of staff. These factors, combined with the opportunity to make better use of surplus accommodation and with changing patterns in the location of pupils in the authority, make a powerful argument for LEAs to review their special schools. If such reviews conclude that rationalisation is necessary, the LEA must act on this, consulting widely and exhibiting an absolute commitment to getting the best value from resources (Section 8).

Schools and teachers should implement practical strategies to improve the quality of learning for pupils with special needs in the classroom

In the new relationship of client and contractor, LEAs and schools will be working in co-operation to achieve the foregoing developments. But there are further issues for schools to address in improving practice in the classroom for pupils with special needs. A major task for schools is to help teachers adopt strategies which are particularly helpful for pupils with special needs, such as differentiating the methods and materials used during lessons, or making available special resources with which these pupils can help themselves (Section 9).

Schools and teachers should plan the use of extra adult support for pupils with special needs

Where extra adult help is provided, planning and communication are the keys to improving its impact. If a small amount of the time currently spent alongside pupils were redirected into planning and discussion about individual pupils between support and classroom teachers, there would be a significant improvement in effectiveness (Section 10).

Schools should include an assessment of achievements with pupils with special needs in the appraisal of teachers

The appraisal of teachers provides an opportunity to ensure that their achievements with pupils with special needs are recognised in the assessment of their overall performance (Section 11).

✳ ✳ ✳

These recommendations are based on the experience of a selection of schools and LEAs. They provide a practical foundation on which all schools and LEAs can build strategies for meeting pupils' special needs.

Introduction

1. In June 1992, the Audit Commission and HMI reported on the situation in England and Wales concerning pupils with special educational needs. As it is estimated that one in six pupils has special needs at any given time, over one million pupils come into this category, accounting in 1990/91 for approximately £1.5 billion expenditure. Almost 170,000 pupils in England and Wales have formal statements of special educational need issued under the 1981 Education Act by LEAs, following multi-disciplinary assessments of the children.

2. Much has been achieved by schools and LEAs in the decade since the passing of the 1981 Education Act, but there are serious deficiencies in the identification of and provision for pupils with special needs. These deficiencies are caused by three problems:

— lack of clarity about what constitutes special educational needs and about the respective responsibilities of schools and LEAs

— lack of accountability by LEAs to parents, by schools and LEAs for the progress made by pupils, and by schools to the LEA for the resources they receive

— lack of incentives for LEAs to implement the 1981 Act.

3. *Getting in on the Act* recommended that guidance should be issued by the Department for Education (DFE) and Welsh Office to define the level of need in a child which should trigger the use of the 1981 Education Act procedures and to help LEAs define the responsibilities of ordinary schools for pupils with special needs. It also recommended that parents of pupils with statements of special need should have rights, within limits, to state a preference for their child's school and to change their child's school. As regards statements, it proposed that they should be changed to focus on the objectives for the child, on the school's responsibilities and to specify the funds to be allocated for the child. It recommended that statutory time limits for all the agencies involved in the completion of assessments and statements should be set, with redress for parents if these are not met and that consideration should be given to introducing a shortened assessment procedure.

4. The report also suggested that consideration should be given to developing incentives for LEAs to implement fully the 1981 Education Act. Regarding the inspection of schools, it proposed that the teams of inspectors planned under the Education (Schools) Act 1992 and existing LEA teams should focus on the schools' work with pupils with special needs and on the progress made by those pupils. Finally it advised that research is needed to assess the provision made for pupils with emotional and behavioural disturbance who are excluded from school.

5. The Government welcomed the Audit Commission/HMI report as stimulating discussion about how the interests of children with special needs could be safeguarded[1]. The relevant local authority associations also welcomed the report[2]. The Government had themselves been review-

---

1   *Department for Education (DFE) press release. 25/6/92.*

2   *Source: correspondence with the Audit Commission/HMI study team.*

ing the provisions of the 1981 Education Act and announced a number of proposals on similar lines in Parliament and in a consultation paper[1]. In particular:

— to consider the development of national criteria on assessments and statements[1]

— to give parents of children with statements the right to express a preference for their child's school[1]

— to regulate the time taken for the completion of assessments and statements[1], and to consult widely on the content and form of regulations that will be required to put this in place, particularly in relation to district health authorities and social services departments and their rôle in the process[2]

— to provide a shorter assessment process where appropriate[2]

— to enable the Secretaries of State for Education and for Wales to amend the relevant Regulations to provide for statements which might set out educational objectives for the child[3].

The Government stated that a number of the proposals could be implemented by amending existing statutory regulations, that some would feature in a White Paper and that others would be the subject of future legislation.

6. In response to a Bill, introduced into the House of Lords by Lord Campbell of Alloway, to set time limits for the completion of statements and to reform the special needs appeals system, the Government announced their intention to reform that appeals system. They have proposed new independent tribunals to hear appeals from parents of children with special needs[1]. The Audit Commission and HMI welcome all these proposals. Further, OHMCI has issued for consultation guidance for the new teams of inspectors planned under the 1992 Education (Schools) Act. This guidance includes advice on how the inspection of schools' provision for pupils with special needs should be conducted[4]. It proposes *inter alia* that inspection teams should report on the academic and social progress made and standards achieved by pupils having learning difficulties.

7. The Government also published a White Paper on education[5] in which they confirmed their proposals outlined in the consultation document, adding that the Secretary of State should be enabled to make regulations providing for more flexible assessment arrangements and for the content and format of statements to be varied. The Government also proposed that once a maintained school is named in a statement, the governors must admit the pupil, that in due course special schools should be given the choice to ballot parents on the case for grant-maintained status and that a new Funding Agency should have rights and duties in the area of special needs alongside LEAs, although LEAs would retain responsibility under the 1981 Education Act for assessing pupils, issuing statements and arranging provision for pupils with statements. The White Paper outlined the Government's intention to give powers to the Secretaries of State for Education and

---

1   *Special Educational Needs – Access to the System. Op.cit.*

2   *Parliamentary Under Secretary of State for Schools. Hansard. 3/7/92.*

3   *Department of Education and Science press release. 11/6/92.*

4   *Framework for the Inspection of Schools. Paper for Consultation. OHMCI. 1992.*

5   *Choice and Diversity. Op.cit.*

for Wales to require LEAs or the Funding Agency to bring forward proposals for the rationalisation of special schools.

8. *Getting in on the Act* also identified steps which schools and LEAs should take to improve the effectiveness of provision for pupils with special needs and these are the subject of this handbook. This handbook does not cover every aspect of provision; its focus is the implementation of the recommendations made in *Getting in on the Act*. A central recommendation is for a clear split between the LEA, as the client in a client/contractor relationship, and the school as the contractor organisation primarily responsible for the delivery of the education of pupils with special needs. The implications of this change are wide-ranging.

9. The distinction between the client and the provider of services offers LEAs the opportunity to develop a rôle as guarantors of the rights of children with special needs and their parents. For many LEAs, this means that greater management attention has to be given to the area of special educational needs. At the same time as they develop systems to call schools to account for their performance with pupils with special needs, LEAs must ensure that they improve their own performance in fulfilling their obligations under the 1981 Education Act. The most pressing improvements are the timely administration of the process of assessing children and issuing statements and attendance at pupils' annual reviews. It would not be credible for LEAs to claim to be champions of children with special needs whilst failing to carry out assessments and issue statements in a timely manner. LEAs must detach themselves from the responsibility of directly providing services to support pupils with special needs, except where no other organisation can provide them. A separation of the rôles of the provider and the regulator is an essential component of effective monitoring.

10. When schools act as contractors, they assume responsibility for fulfilling the potential of pupils with special needs. The resources to do the job should be clearly specified by LEAs and delegated to schools. The task which schools must address and the resources to help them achieve it will then be clearly defined.

11. Hand in hand with delegation goes accountability. Schools should expect to have their performance and use of resources monitored more closely than has been the case to date, giving schools an incentive to achieve progress with pupils with special needs.

12. There will also be increased accountability to parents. The recommendation to give parents of pupils with statements the right to state a preference for their child's school – and particularly to state a preference for a change of school – is likely to reinforce the trend for an increasing proportion of children with special needs to be placed in ordinary schools. The survey of parents conducted during the study of the national situation revealed that 36% of parents of pupils in special schools wanted to change their child's school, usually to an ordinary school[1].

13. This trend raises questions about the future of special schools. Special schools continue to be required not only for those pupils for whom ordinary schools cannot provide, but also to provide choice for parents. But falling rolls, surplus accommodation and the requirement to deliver the National Curriculum all combine to make a review of special schools essential for LEAs. It is particularly important as LEAs are required to draw up schemes for local management

---

1   *Op. cit. pages 30-31.*

7

of special schools by September 1993 for implementation in April 1994. LEAs must decide how many special school places they should fund. This cannot be done properly without reference to the facilities which are available in ordinary schools for providing for pupils with special needs. LEAs should take early soundings of parental preferences as these must be a guiding principle in any rationalisation proposals.

14. The handbook is divided into two parts: the first deals primarily with the 'client' rôle of the LEA and its practical implications for schools, which will be asked by LEAs to implement a number of the strategies outlined. Schools will have responsibilities to fulfil alongside LEAs. The second part of the handbook considers three further issues for schools and teachers to address in improving the quality of learning in the classroom for pupils with special needs. Each section ends with a checklist for schools and LEAs to use to highlight the actions required by them.

15. If the developments and the strategies detailed in this handbook are to contribute to an improvement in effectiveness, each LEA and school should have a policy which ensures that the direction in which the organisation is heading is clear and that individual strategies form part of a coherent whole. The special needs policy is therefore the starting point of this management handbook (Exhibit 1).

Exhibit 1
IMPROVING THE MANAGEMENT OF SPECIAL NEEDS PROVISION
The special needs policy is the starting point for implementing a range of strategies

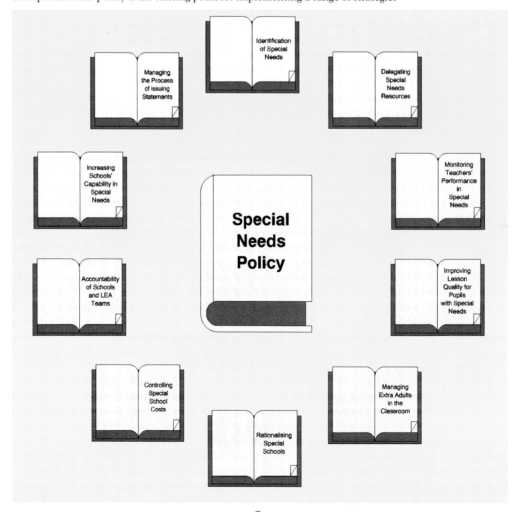

8

Part One:
Champions of Children with Special Needs?

A rôle for LEAs and schools in co-operation

1. The Special Needs Policy

16. A special needs policy is the foundation for strategies to help pupils with special needs achieve their educational potential. A policy without strategies of the type outlined in this handbook is merely a statement of good intentions, but implementing strategies without the coherence which a policy should provide risks different parts of the service pulling in different directions. The basic features of a special needs policy are similar for both LEAs and schools, although different indicators will be used to measure the impact of the policy. School and LEA policies are dealt with together in this section. School policies should interrelate with the LEA's special needs policy. Elected members should ensure that the LEA policy is set, and governors that the school policy is set.

17. The best special needs policies are short, clear documents which are set in the context of the LEA's policy for the whole education service and include the following features to focus attention on the intended outcome of the policy:

— a description of the client groups to whom the policy applies

— a statement of the principles on which the LEA or school will develop its provision for pupils with special needs

— the LEA's or school's objectives, expressed in terms of the anticipated benefits of the policy for pupils with special needs and their parents

— the timescale over which the objectives should be achieved

— an outline of the priorities for the allocation of resources

— the indicators to be used to monitor the implementation of the policy.

LEAs should consider providing for parents a summary of the principles on which provision for pupils with special needs is being developed. Clwyd LEA, for example, introduces its handbook explaining the rights of parents of children with special needs, and the services provided for them, with such a summary (Box A, overleaf).

18. The policy should also take into account the provisions of the 1988 Education Reform Act that the curriculum for maintained schools must specify the 'matters, skills and processes' which are to be taught to pupils of different abilities. The policy should not detail all the strategies and facilities which will be developed to achieve the LEA's aims. It can be used as the basis on which the LEA sets the number of staff it will retain for functions such as educational psychology and special needs advice. LEAs will be required by the DFE and Welsh Office to produce a detailed outline of their policies and strategies in this area as part of their proposals for local management of special schools[1].

---

1   *Circular 7/91 in England and 38/91 in Wales.*

CLWYD LEA's STATEMENT OF PRINCIPLES FOR PROVIDING FOR PUPILS WITH SPECIAL NEEDS
Clwyd's handbook for parents of children with special needs outlines the principles and objectives of the LEA in this area

> ‘ **THE SPECIAL EDUCATION SERVICES SEEK TO ENSURE:**
>
> ‘ that all children with special educational needs (as defined in the 1981 Education Act), whether physical, intellectual, social or emotional, receive appropriate educational provision whatever the extent of need. It is expected that such provision will enable them to overcome their problems as far as possible and to develop their potential to the maximum. Satisfactory assimilation into the community is the ultimate aim
>
> ‘ that each child's special educational needs are identified and recorded, and that regular reviews are made of progress
>
> ‘ that individual programmes, objectives and targets are set so that suitable curriculum provision is made for each child to proceed at an appropriate level of development
>
> ‘ that wherever it is considered possible and desirable, each child's special educational needs are provided for in an ordinary school alongside his/her peers
>
> ‘ that there are comprehensive support services, including advisory staff in special education, a schools' psychological service, a special needs support service, a partially hearing service and educational social workers
>
> ‘ that short term and part-time withdrawal facilities for individual children are provided at area based assessment and remedial centres
>
> ‘ that specialist schools are available for pupils whose needs will be most appropriately met in these settings. ’

Source: Clwyd LEA's handbook for parents of children with special needs.

19. LEA and school special needs policies should include a statement of the indicators which will be used to monitor the implementation of the policy. Indicators highlight to elected members and school governors the impact of the policy and suggest when corrective action is necessary. Indicators should focus on a few key trends. Lincolnshire LEA provides a helpful example of this (Box B). Such indicators are only of use if the original policy objectives are themselves measurable. For example, Lincolnshire LEA's objective to place in ordinary schools the majority of pupils with statements issued because of learning difficulties is capable of measurement.

20. Indicators which compare the take-up of services with the resources provided for those services are particularly helpful because they highlight areas where resources are not being rationalised in line with changes in demand. For example, monitoring the pupil:adult ratio in special schools will highlight cases where pupils are moving out of special schools but staffing resources are not being reallocated accordingly.

21. Indicators can be quantitative, as in Lincolnshire, or qualitative. For example, LEAs could aggregate grades for the quality of learning for pupils with special needs given by inspectors

POLICY PERFORMANCE INDICATORS IN LINCOLNSHIRE
In Lincolnshire, the elected members of the LEA review the LEA's performance in special needs using a number of key indicators

> Lincolnshire LEA's special needs policy sets out objectives for the special needs service. One of them is to place an increasing proportion of pupils with moderate learning difficulties in ordinary schools until the majority are educated there. Services which increase the capability of ordinary schools in educating pupils with special needs are a priority for resources. Progress in the implementation of the policy is measured by the following indicators:
>
> **Pupil numbers** in ordinary and special schools and special units
>
> **Occupancy rates** of special schools and units
>
> **Pupil: teacher ratios**
>
> **Number of support staff in ordinary schools**
>
> **Number of pupils with statements**
>
> **Placement of pupils with statements**
>
> **Special school expenditure per pupil**
>
> **Expenditure per pupil in special units**
>
> **Expenditure on placements outside the LEA.**
>
> Each indicator is presented in a table showing trends over the last four years, enabling the elected members of the LEA to see the direction of change. Trends are also presented graphically. The Director of Education makes an annual report to members on the progress made in implementing the policy. This report opens with a single paragraph which details the progress made in two or three important areas and ends with a detailed breakdown of the above statistics.

during observations of pupils in lessons. This would indicate to elected members whether, for example, a policy of placing an increasing proportion of pupils with special needs in ordinary schools was resulting in an improvement in the quality of learning for them. A number of such indicators are described in this handbook. Although these are presented in the context of calling individual schools to account for their work in special needs, they can be aggregated to provide a picture at LEA level of the impact of the special needs policy.

22. Schools need different indicators of the impact of their policy, for example:

— the number of pupils receiving extra help

— the rate of progress of pupils since extra help was given

— the proportion of school funds spent on special needs

— the proportion of pupils' timetables which involves them in ordinary classes.

These indicators will enable school governors, who have very limited time, to get a snapshot of the impact of schools' special needs policies. The school development plan will encapsulate the strategies for achieving progress in these areas.

23. An annual report ensures that elected members' or governors' attention is drawn to the need to adjust the policy in the light of changes in circumstances. Lincolnshire, for example, has adjusted its special needs policy on several occasions since 1985 in the light of changes in legislation in other areas of education. In such circumstances, LEAs and schools must also adjust the performance indicators, to ensure that they reflect revisions in the policy.

*   *   *

24. Once the policy and the arrangements for monitoring its implementation have been set, schools and LEAs should develop strategies for the management of each component part of the service. The rest of this handbook provides an outline of good management practice on which LEAs and schools can build strategies for the delivery of provision for pupils with special needs.

CHECKLIST FOR ACTION – THE SPECIAL NEEDS POLICY

Action by LEAs	Action by schools	Action by both	Already in place?	Action required?
LEA sets a special needs policy				
	Governors set special needs policy			
		Policy has all the essential components (paragraph 17)		
		Policy includes qualitative and quantitative indicators		
Annual report made to members				
	Annual report made to governors			
		Policy reviewed to reflect changes and indicators changed accordingly		

Source: Audit Commission/HMI.

2. The Identification of Pupils with Special Educational Needs

25. *Getting in on the Act* highlighted inconsistencies between and within schools and LEAs in the identification of pupils with special educational needs. Schools require guidance on the level of need in a child which should trigger the provision of extra attention and on the threshold at which they can expect the LEA to help with pupils with special needs and initiate multi-disciplinary assessments. The report recommended that the DFE and Welsh Office should issue national guidelines to indicate when pupils should be assessed formally under the 1981 Education Act. But local guidelines will also be required to take account of LEAs' individual schemes for local management of schools and to ensure consistency between schools in the identification of the large majority of pupils with special needs who do not require a formal assessment.

26. The LEA is responsible for drawing up local guidelines to encourage the consistent identification of pupils with special needs and will need to ensure that the local guidelines reflect the proposed national guidelines. Both LEA- and grant-maintained schools should be involved in the process. As the LEA also has responsibility for pupils placed in grant-maintained schools whose special needs cannot be met by the ordinarily available provision outlined in the guidance, it is important that the thresholds for providing pupils with extra help are applied consistently in both types of school. Involving schools gives the guidelines credibility in the eyes of head teachers, and helps ensure that it is practicable for schools to implement them.

27. Guidelines can be used to identify the incidence of pupils with special needs in different schools and hence as a basis for distributing special needs funds to schools through formula funding. The use of guidelines in this context is considered later (Section 5). Guidelines have an educational value in improving the consistency with which pupils' special needs are identified.

28. The principal task is to draw up guidelines which are not so prescriptive as to exclude pupils whose special needs do not fit into categories and yet not so general as to include too large a proportion of pupils, thereby spreading finite resources too thinly. The Warnock Committee's[1] estimate that at a given time one in six pupils has special educational needs has been widely accepted.   Although LEAs may designate a larger proportion of the pupil population as having

---

1   *The Report of the Committee of Enquiry into the Education of Handicapped Children and Young People. HMSO. 1978.*

special needs, there are limits under the formula funding of schools[1] on the total amount of funds which can be allocated to schools on the basis of pupils with special needs without statements, although in practice a greater limitation is usually the proportion of the education budget which LEAs allocate to special needs. If an LEA targets limited resources at a greater number of pupils, each pupil with special needs will bring smaller amounts of extra funding, making it difficult for the school to provide significant additional help for them.

29. Some LEAs have already implemented strategies to ensure greater consistency in the identification of pupils with special needs without statements, and a few are piloting guidelines on the level of special need which should trigger registration of a child for extra attention. Clwyd is one LEA where schools and the LEA have experience in improving the identification of pupils with special needs (Box C). As in Clwyd, guidelines for schools on the identification of pupils with special needs should refer to the level of need in a child. It is not enough to say that children should be identified as having special needs which trigger additional funding only because the school finds it difficult to cope with them. This would create a perverse incentive for schools to fail to provide fully for pupils with special needs.

30. Registers can reflect different degrees of need by operating at several levels with, for example, pupils with the lowest level of need being the responsibility of the school alone and pupils at a higher level triggering the allocation of funds to the school through the formula. It could be argued that such systems reward schools which do not succeed, on the grounds that if the school fails to make progress with a pupil eventually the pupil will proceed to a higher level on the register and the school will gain additional funding. To counterbalance any such tendency, the LEA should have a system for monitoring schools' work with these pupils. LEA advisers or educational psychologists should ask the school to outline what strategies they are attempting and to provide indicators of the progress which the pupil is making. On occasions the adviser or educational psychologist will observe the child in class. Thereby the LEA can satisfy itself that schools are fulfilling their responsibilities before gaining additional resources from the LEA.

31. When additional resources result from the identification of pupils as having special needs, entry onto the register should be validated externally to schools to ensure consistency. Some LEAs have found, not surprisingly, that some schools artificially inflate the number of pupils with special needs, causing the register to lose credibility. The cost of external moderation is not great. In Clwyd, for example, the validation of schools' requests to have children put on the register is carried out twice yearly by advisory and support teachers visiting each school. The administration of the register for all schools in the LEA takes slightly less than half of one clerical officer's time. Clwyd has almost 6,500 pupils (16% of the maintained school population) on its special needs register. Reviewing the progress of pupils on the register and ensuring that the register is up-to-date is undertaken by educational psychologists and advisory and support teachers spending half a day every six months in each school.

---

1   *From April 1993 the limits will be as follows: LEAs may allocate up to 5% of the Aggregated Schools Budget on the basis of additional weightings to the basic unit of pupil funding. They may allocate further amounts for special needs on the basis of other factors, up to a limit of 20% of the Aggregated Schools Budget. They may also allocate funds for work with pupils with special needs from that part of the Potential Schools Budget, to be introduced from 1993 onwards, which they have decided to retain centrally rather than delegate to schools. At least 85% of the Potential Schools Budget will have to be delegated to schools.*

Box C
THE IDENTIFICATION OF PUPILS WITH SPECIAL NEEDS IN CLWYD
Clwyd has developed a register of pupils with special needs and is now piloting guidelines for the entry of pupils onto it

Schools in Clwyd use a county-wide register of pupils with special educational needs but without a statement. The register, originally designed to encourage primary school teachers systematically to identify pupils with special needs, forms part of the LEA's scheme for the local management of schools (LMS). The register has two levels which relate to the severity of need in the child. Entry onto the first level of the register is a mark of a school's concern for a child experiencing difficulty in learning. A child can only be registered following discussion between the school and an LEA representative – usually the educational psychologist. Schools provide the extra help for pupils on level one of the register.

Level two of the register is for pupils with more severe special needs. The LEA is currently piloting guidelines for teachers which indicate the level of need in a child which triggers inclusion at level two. These guidelines are the outcome of co-operation between the LEA and head teachers. They do not outline rigid categories of special need, but give schools a measure with which to assess whether a child's difficulties are severe enough to trigger the provision of extra help from the LEA. The guidelines are expressed in terms of the minimum level of ability which a pupil in a given year should have. Pupils achieving below this level are considered to have special needs sufficient to warrant entry on to level two of the register. For example:

'Pupils in Year 4. A child should:

— **be no more than 9 months behind his or her chronological age in reading (New Neale's Analysis Test)**

— **be no more than 15 months behind in spelling (Young's Parallel Spelling Test)**

— **be able to narrate experiences**

— **be able to achieve National Curriculum Level 2 Mathematics**

— **show no problems with fine motor skills.'**

These are a selection of some 18 areas of functioning in which teachers in Clwyd are given guidance on the level of need in a child which triggers entry to level two of the register. The guidelines are naturally different for pupils of different ages.

Clwyd LEA wishes to ensure that schools fulfil their own responsibilities for pupils with special needs, particularly in the case of pupils with behavioural problems where a great deal may depend on the school's willingness to attempt different strategies to manage difficult behaviour. In the case of pupils with emotional or behavioural disturbances, schools have to satisfy three additional conditions:

'The school must demonstrate that they have:

1. maintained the child in a mainstream setting

2. allowed the child maximum access to the curriculum

3. pursued a programme to help the child modify his or her behaviour.'

Entry to level two of the register attracts additional funding for the school. The LEA has to agree that entry to this level is merited, and, as with entry to level one, this is done by educational psychologists who independently assess whether a child's level of need is broadly consistent with the pilot guidelines.

32. One consequence of encouraging schools to identify pupils with special needs is that the total number of pupils so identified is likely to increase in the short term. This happened in Clwyd (Exhibit 2), and in other LEAs which have used registers of pupils with special needs. Clwyd experienced a sharp rise in the number of pupils registered shortly before the implementation of local management of schools, as head teachers sought to secure additional funding in respect of these pupils. This prompted Clwyd to introduce written guidelines in the year 1990/91 for entry onto the register in order to ensure that resources were targeted consistently at the most needy pupils. Prior to this, the LEA had used only informal guidelines. The trend in the number of pupils on Clwyd's register suggests that the LEA is managing to stabilise the situation. If such short-term increases are not managed by LEAs, then the registers and guidelines lose credibility because, where they are used as the basis for allocating funds to schools, the available resources are spread over so many pupils that their impact is diluted.

Exhibit 2
THE NUMBER OF PUPILS ON CLWYD'S REGISTER OF SPECIAL NEEDS
After a period of rapid growth, the LEA introduced clearer guidelines in 1991 which helped to stabilise the number of pupils on the register

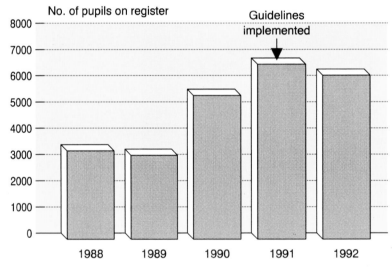

Source: Audit Commission/HMI fieldwork.

20

CHECKLIST FOR ACTION – THE IDENTIFICATION OF PUPILS WITH SPECIAL NEEDS

Action by LEAs	Action by schools	Action by both	Already in place?	Action required?
Guidelines on levels of need in children which trigger extra help are drawn up				
	LEA- and grant-maintained schools contribute to guidelines and methods for implementing them			
Guidelines use criteria which are objective and vary with pupils' ages				
		Guidelines outline schools' responsibilities and threshold at which LEA will provide help		
	System is implemented			
Schools' requests for pupils to be registered are moderated to ensure that they are consistent with guidelines				
Staff are tasked with verifying that schools have fulfilled their own responsibilities prior to allocation of additional funds from LEA				

Source: Audit Commission/HMI.

3. Increasing the Capability of Ordinary Schools

33. The 1981 Education Act requires LEAs to place pupils in ordinary schools subject to certain conditions. LEAs should increase the capability of ordinary schools to provide for pupils with special needs. Such a strategy is likely to include practical help in establishing teaching practice appropriate for pupils with special needs and specific projects, for example setting up a library of teaching materials for pupils with special educational needs. It may include the support of an individual pupil in an ordinary school to enable a school to overcome a short-term difficulty with a pupil. However, the main aim is to increase the capability of ordinary schools so that they are able to provide for pupils with special needs from their own resources. The help can be provided by the LEA or other qualified organisations, such as voluntary bodies or special schools. Nottinghamshire LEA illustrates one way in which a strategy of this kind can be implemented (Box D, overleaf).

34. Clear communication of priorities will leave schools in no doubt as to the circumstances in which the LEA will help them develop their special needs provision. This confirms their own responsibilities and makes the process of allocation fair. Lack of clarity in the basis on which competing requests for resources are dealt with is the source of frustration to schools. Many LEAs, including Nottinghamshire, share decisions about the allocation of resources to schools with head teachers to reduce the risk of such frustration. The cost of the joint decision making process in Nottinghamshire is approximately 36 person-days annually for each of eight LEA area offices – half provided by the LEA and half by schools. However, Nottinghamshire is a large LEA with approximately 145,000 maintained pupils. LEAs with smaller populations would have proportionately fewer schools for which to administer the scheme and may not need area meetings of LEA officers and head teachers, as one group may suffice for the whole LEA.

35. The cost of such systems is also offset to some degree by reductions in the time previously spent by head teachers and LEA officers in managing special needs resources under the old system, and in the time spent resolving conflicts over funding and by the greater rigour with which the need for resources is reviewed, resulting in more recycling of resources. This recycling of resources arises because the LEA delegates responsibility for reviewing the need for resources allocated to schools to local groups of head teachers and LEA officers. They are closer to schools and more able to evaluate requests for the continuation of resources than headquarters staff who may be remote from the 'front line'. To maximise the reallocation of resources, some allocations to schools in Nottinghamshire are reviewed termly rather than annually.

INCREASING THE CAPABILITY OF NOTTINGHAMSHIRE'S ORDINARY SCHOOLS TO PROVIDE FOR PUPILS WITH SPECIAL NEEDS
Nottinghamshire targeted its special needs resources to increase teachers' skills and ordinary schools' facilities for pupils with special needs

In January 1989, the inspection service in Nottinghamshire LEA surveyed the provision made for 44 pupils with special educational needs. It identified a number of deficiencies and this was the trigger for a full review of the LEA's policy for pupils with special needs. In 1990, the LEA introduced a new policy, entitled 'Children First'. In pursuit of the policy, the LEA implemented a strategy to increase the capability of ordinary schools to provide for pupils with special needs. The LEA concentrated initially on provision for pupils with moderate learning difficulties.

In 1990/91 Nottinghamshire allocated part of a £336,000 development fund and all of its special needs support teams to this task – resources totalling some £3 million out of a total education budget of £388 million. It communicated clearly to all schools the priorities for the allocation of these resources. Priority was to be given to pupils with statements, to pupils with the most significant needs, and to schools intending to improve their practice in this area.

Nottinghamshire decided that the LEA should not be the sole arbiter of schools' requests for resources. It set up local groups, comprising head teachers and LEA officers tasked with allocating resources to schools. Head teachers therefore felt that decisions would be made by peers who had an understanding of their problems. Schools now submit proposals for the use of those resources to the 'Mainstream Support Groups', as they are called. The resources include money, non-teaching assistants and qualified special needs teachers. Proposals from schools range from requests for individual support for pupils experiencing a temporary difficulty to joint requests from secondary schools and their feeder primary schools to set up programmes of special help for pupils with special needs in primary schools which can be continued by the secondary school when the pupils transfer. The local groups also allocate resources for pupils with statements.

Requests for formal assessments under the 1981 Education Act are closely examined by the educational psychology service to make sure that schools have attempted strategies to provide for these pupils, using the resources of the Mainstream Support Groups, before passing the legal responsibility for determining the child's education to the LEA through the 1981 Act.

The LEA decided that two important indicators of the success of the policy were the numbers of pupils (i) requiring places in special schools for pupils with moderate learning difficulties and (ii) receiving statements. The former indicates the degree to which ordinary schools are taking on pupils who would previously have gone to special schools, and the latter the degree to which schools provide for pupils from within ordinarily available provision and using the resources of the Mainstream Support Groups.

Nottinghamshire plans to repeat its inspection of provision for pupils with special needs in ordinary schools to inform its evaluation of the impact of its strategy on the quality of learning for pupils with special needs.

36. Funding for such strategies may come from the LEA's centrally retained funds. Funds can also be delegated to schools through the formula. In particular, funds for the support of individual pupils can be delegated. A number of LEAs do so already and all LEAs should consider doing so.

37. The LEA should not insist that schools receive help to build up their expertise only from the LEA itself. LEAs should be principally in the rôle of the client in a client/contractor relationship with schools. They should leave schools free to purchase resources from the organisation which offers them the best value for money, for example under an annual agreement. In many cases this will be with the LEA's own teams of advisers or support teachers, but LEAs should not use their influence to distort schools' purchasing decisions. LEAs could consider the example of Cumbria LEA which is setting up a scheme to approve a number of organisations, such as voluntary groups, special schools and its own advisory teams, which are capable of helping schools in the area of special educational needs. Schools may then choose the organisation to provide the service funded by the LEA. In this way, even when resources are not formally delegated through the formula, schools can exercise choice in selecting organisations which in their opinion can best help them.

38. Increasing the capability of ordinary schools is likely to have an impact beyond ordinary schools. In Nottinghamshire, for example, the number of pupils in special schools for pupils with moderate learning difficulties began to fall as a significant number of pupils continued or were placed in ordinary schools when they would otherwise have gone to special schools (Exhibit 3). It is important therefore that LEAs' information systems highlight such developments, so that the LEA can take action – in this case, ensuring that resources are reallocated in line with changes in the pupil population. This is the subject of a separate section (Section 7).

Exhibit 3
THE IMPACT OF INCREASING THE CAPABILITY OF ORDINARY SCHOOLS IN NOTTINGHAMSHIRE
Nottinghamshire's 'Children First' policy (Box D) accelerated the decline in the number of pupils in special schools for pupils with moderate learning difficulties (MLD)

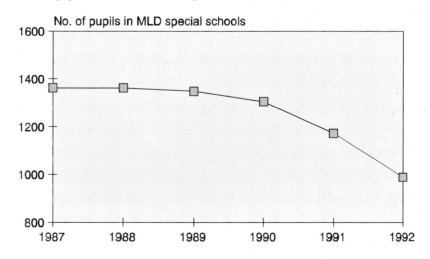

Source: Audit Commission/HMI fieldwork.

39. If such a strategy is implemented successfully, there should normally be a decrease in the number of statements which an LEA issues, as a general increase in schools' skills with pupils with special needs means that a greater number of pupils can be provided for from provision which is ordinarily available. The number of statements issued annually by Nottinghamshire decreased accordingly (Exhibit 4). A decrease in the number of statements which arises from such strategies, rather than from a failure properly to administer the 1981 Act, is compatible with the intent of that Act that statements should only be issued for pupils whose needs cannot be met through generally available provision. Such a decrease is by no means always a positive performance indicator as it could also be a sign of increasing delays in the administration of the process of issuing statements. LEAs must ensure that they continue to assess pupils in ordinary schools whose needs fall within the proposed national guidelines and issue statements where appropriate. It is unlikely that any LEA will reach a point where statements are no longer required for any pupils in ordinary schools.

Exhibit 4
TREND IN THE NUMBER OF STATEMENTS ISSUED IN NOTTINGHAMSHIRE
The LEA issued fewer statements as it began to implement its policy of increasing the capability of ordinary schools with pupils with special needs

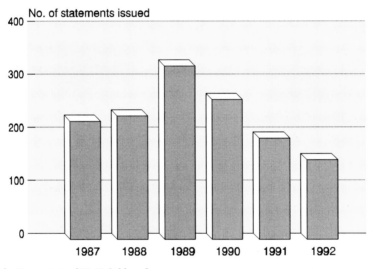

Source: Audit Commission/HMI fieldwork

40. Increasing the capability of ordinary schools will not lead to a decrease in the number of statements issued if the LEA has a large backlog of statements which should continue to be issued. Also, the number of statements will not reduce if the LEA does not plan for schools continuing to push for statements to be issued despite the increase in their capability with pupils with special needs. Schools see statements as a means of getting additional resources, which is an incentive for them to refer cases. For example, another study LEA also increased the skills of its ordinary schools, but in this LEA the number of statements issued increased (Exhibit 5). The difference between this LEA and Nottinghamshire is that in Nottinghamshire the educational psychology service had a clearer rôle in ensuring that schools had made all reasonable attempts to help a pupil make progress before agreeing to a referral for a multi-disciplinary assessment.

Exhibit 5
TREND IN NUMBER OF STATEMENTS ISSUED IN TWO LEAs
The different trends are explained by the different degrees to which the LEAs ensured that schools had fulfilled their responsibilities

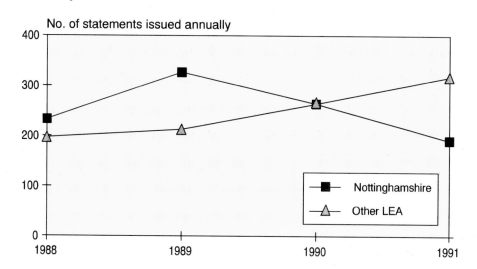

Source: *Audit Commission/HMI fieldwork in two LEAs*

41. There will be occasions when the school and educational psychologist disagree, as not all schools accept responsibility for providing for pupils with special needs to the same degree. Although the chief educational psychologists in some LEAs are reluctant to take on the rôle of ensuring that schools have fulfilled their responsibilities, it is very difficult for the LEA to implement the 1981 Act consistently across all its schools if this is not done by the educational psychologists or by other officers of the LEA.

42. The inability of a school to cater for a pupil with special needs may not be due to a lack of skill, but to a lack of facilities. A number of LEAs have undertaken programmes of investment in ordinary schools, costing between one and two per cent of the LEA special needs budget. Where the pupils targeted for placement in such specially resourced ordinary schools are pupils who are, or would be, placed in independent or non-maintained special schools, then the investment can be partly offset by savings in school fees. It may take several years to recoup the costs of such 'pump-priming' as there is a time lag between the facilities being created and fully occupied, because it might be too disruptive to move pupils out of their existing schools part way through their school career. Hence these new places may be filled principally with appropriate pupils from each year's new intake. There will be a similar time lag if pupils are placed there from the LEA's own special schools, as LEAs may have to wait until the end of a school year to undertake some rationalisation of staffing to release the resources from the special schools (Exhibit 6, overleaf). The potential for recouping investment is only one factor to be taken into account. Many LEAs undertake such developments as part of their commitment to improving facilities for disabled children and young people.

Exhibit 6
RECOUPING THE COST OF PROVIDING SPECIAL FACILITIES IN ORDINARY SCHOOLS (ILLUSTRATIVE EXAMPLE)
Investments in improving the facilities of ordinary schools can be recouped, to some degree at least, by savings in special school costs

Year	Activity	Investment in facilities	New savings from this year's placements	Total annual savings this year	Cumulative savings
0	LEA adapts ordinary school to take 8 pupils with disabilities including restricted mobility. Three places allocated for year 1. Reductions in special school staffing scheduled accordingly	£100,000			
1	Two places filled by pupils who would otherwise have gone to LEA special schools and 1 by pupil who would otherwise have gone to non-maintained special school. Five places allocated for year 2. LEA pays for 1.5 non-teaching assistants (NTAs)		School fees of £18,000 saved. Reduced LEA special school staffing saves £16,000. Deduct cost of NTAs and pupil funding: £13,000 saved	£13,000	£13,000
2	Three places filled by pupils who would otherwise have gone to LEA special schools and 2 by pupils who would otherwise have gone to non-maintained special schools. 3.5 additional NTAs funded by LEA		School fees of £36,000 saved. Special school staffing reduced by £24,000. Deduct cost of NTAs and pupil funding: £15,000 saved	£28,000	£41,000
3	All places occupied			£28,000	£69,000
4	All places occupied			£28,000	£97,000

CHECKLIST FOR ACTION – INCREASING THE CAPABILITY OF ORDINARY SCHOOLS

Action by LEAs	Action by schools	Action by both	Already in place?	Action required?
		Schools' capabilities to meet special needs are established		
Strategy for improving schools' capabilities is designed				
Priorities for allocation of resources are publicised to schools				
		System for allocating resources involves schools		
	Proposals for use of resources to increase special needs capability are put forward			
		System to review continued need for resources is implemented		
Indicators of the impact of the strategy on ordinary and special schools are defined				
Rôle of educational psychology service in evaluating requests for formal assessments is defined				
		Ordinary schools are identified for provision of specialist facilities for pupils with special needs		

Source: Audit Commission/HMI.

4. Managing the Process of Assessment and Issuing Statements

43. Delays in assessing children and issuing statements are a major cause of dissatisfaction among parents and head teachers. Delays make information provided by assessments out of date and reduce their usefulness as a basis on which to set objectives for the child. LEAs should examine whether the cause of delay arises from inefficient administrative systems, such as seeking advice consecutively from the professionals involved rather than simultaneously, or from a lack of managerial supervision.

44. It should not be assumed that delays are due to a lack of staff to perform the function. LEAs with similar turn-around times expend significantly different amounts of administrative time on each statement. Among the study LEAs there was a small minority where an increase in the number of staff employed, especially at peak times, would have reduced the backlog. Unfortunately, as most LEAs do not plot trends in their backlog of cases, they cannot tell if the backlog is getting better or worse. These LEAs should gather data on the backlog of cases awaiting completion in addition to implementing the actions recommended in this section.

45. Most LEAs have periods of peak demand for assessments – in particular, the end of the autumn term. A school may take at least a term to identify which pupils in the new intake have special needs and to attempt strategies to meet those needs from their own resources; consequently many schools refer pupils for multi-disciplinary assessments at the end of the first term. The second common peak time is the second half of the summer term. LEAs often experience a peak of referrals from primary schools in respect of pupils who will be moving to secondary school at the start of the next academic year.

46. This peak is avoidable. In many cases the primary schools have been aware for some time that a pupil may require formal assessment but have neglected to make a timely formal referral. By delaying, they prevent the LEA from completing the multi-disciplinary assessment until the next academic year, when the professionals involved have the next opportunity to assess the child in school. Secondary schools complain that too many pupils arrive without a completed statement and without extra help at a time when they particularly need it, having just transferred to a new environment. All schools visited in the study complained at the length of time taken by LEAs to complete statements. Schools themselves should make prompt referrals. LEAs should issue guidelines to schools to make it clear that referrals made in the final half-term of the year should be exceptional.

47. Schools should be aware that a referral for assessment does not automatically result in an assessment. It is for the LEA in conjunction with parents to decide whether an assessment is

appropriate and, under the Government's proposals, parents will have rights of appeal if they disagree with the LEA's decision.

48. Other organisations, notably district health authorities, also have a part to play with LEAs in ensuring timely completion of the process of issuing statements. The Government have decided that comprehensive provision must be made for regulating the time and the way in which local education authorities carry out the process and have stated that they will consult on the content and form of the regulations that will be required to put this in place, particularly in relation to district health authorities and social services departments and their rôle in the process[1]. Some LEAs have already agreed with their local health authorities that the latter should provide advice to the LEA within a specified time. For the moment, LEAs should work on the principle that six weeks is a reasonable timescale for the receipt of the medical advice, providing that the parents ensure that their child turns up for appointments.

49. However, the factor which distinguishes the LEAs with the fastest turn-around times is the greater amount of time spent in overseeing the process by the chief educational psychologists and senior LEA officers responsible. These LEAs set personal targets for those involved – a common managerial strategy, to which the process of issuing statements lends itself. Another factor is the commitment of senior managers to providing incentives for staff to meet targets. In Solihull, for example, this is visible in the publication of performance measures and the inclusion of the achievement of target times in the performance appraisal of those involved (Box E). To achieve an overall target, objectives should be set for the component parts of the process (Exhibit 7, overleaf). The Government propose to implement statutory time limits for each stage of the process[2]. Until they do so, LEAs should consider setting targets for the decision on whether to proceed with assessment, sending requests for professional advice, the receipt of professional advice, the agreement of a school placement with parents and the issuing of the draft and final statements.

50. To be effective, targets must be achievable and within the control of the people who have to meet them. There should be scope for renegotiation of targets if circumstances change – for example, if there is an unexpected fluctuation in referrals.

51. Timely completion of statements need not result in a lowering of their quality. In fact, in the faster LEAs, a slightly higher proportion of statements than in other LEAs were based on advice which was specific, focused on the objectives for the child and the provision specified by the LEA related more clearly to the needs of the child. Further, timeliness is an essential component of quality since the value of the assessment decreases with delay.

52. An important part of the process of assessment is the contribution of parents to the process. Some LEAs go to considerable lengths to secure this. In Leeds, for example, an LEA officer visits parents at home prior to the commencement of the assessment, and sometimes there is a further visit from the educational psychologist, a practice common to many LEAs. Lincolnshire also achieves a high rate of response from parents, with over 75% of them contributing in writing at some stage during the process. The LEA achieves this by an efficient process of

1   Parliamentary Under Secretary of State for Schools. Hansard. 3/7/92.

2   Special Educational Needs – Access to the System. Op. cit.

SETTING TARGETS FOR THE COMPLETION OF STATEMENTS IN SOLIHULL
The LEA monitors the performance of key individuals involved in the process

Solihull LEA emphasises the responsibility of individuals to achieve tasks within defined times. The LEA sets targets for each of the LEA officers involved in multi-disciplinary assessments of pupils with special needs.

These targets are published and form part of the personal appraisal of managers of the service. Targets are then reinforced by the production of performance indicators highlighting individuals' performance against target. For example, the educational psychology service had a target to complete the production of professional advice within three weeks of receiving the request. To allow for situations where a child may be ill, for example, the service was set an objective of completing 90% of statutory assessments within the target time. It managed to achieve this in the academic year 1990/91.

Solihull now finds that it needs to adjust some of its targets as demand has increased and the pattern of referral has changed. To avoid setting the service impossible targets, the LEA is considering changing the target time to six weeks. Comparing Solihull's staffing levels with other LEAs, it has a ratio of one educational psychologist to 4,600 maintained pupils, close to the median for the 12 LEAs studied.

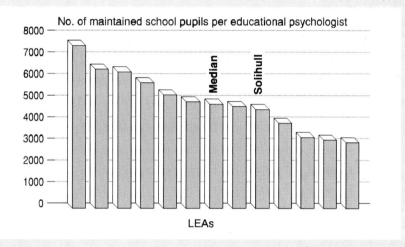

No. of maintained school pupils per educational psychologist

The educational psychology service is also able to renegotiate the completion date of an individual assessment if the achievement of the target time is outside its control, for example when a referral arises during the holidays or when a child is in hospital and it is essential for the child to be observed in school.

The officer responsible for the administration of the process has the objective of issuing a draft statement within three months of notifying the parents of the LEA's intention to assess their child.

The LEA has negotiated target times with the district health authority and has had consistently better response times from the medical officer than other LEAs.

The targets set by the LEA have on occasions been difficult to achieve because of a sudden increase in the number of referrals for formal assessments by primary schools at the end of the year, as schools try to complete outstanding matters before the summer holiday. The LEA is now working with schools to encourage them to refer all pupils for whom a multi-disciplinary assessment appears necessary by Easter.

In a number of cases where the LEA and parents are in agreement, Solihull manages to issue statements within 4.5 months from the date of the decision to assess the child.

Exhibit 7
TARGETS FOR THE COMPLETION OF STATEMENTS
Objectives should be set for the component parts of the process

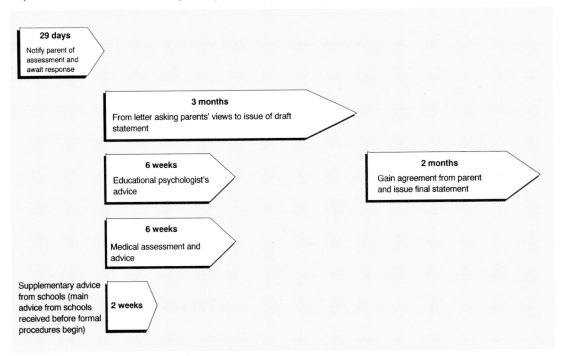

Source: Audit Commission/HMI fieldwork in Solihull LEA

follow-up of parents who do not respond. Schools also have a part to play in encouraging parents to contribute to assessments as they will have frequent contact with the parents.

53. Where, during the assessment, an LEA is considering on social rather than educational grounds a placement for a child which involves him or her living away from home, it should ensure that there is close liaison with the social services department. Local authorities as a whole have obligations under the 1989 Children Act to promote the well-being of children in need, and the practice of different departments in relation to children with special educational needs should be consistent. This liaison is particularly important in the case of children who may be placed in residential provision, but should take place in all cases where children are deemed by the local authority to be in need under the 1989 Children Act.

54. The take-up of computer systems for the administration of statements has been slow – and yet it is a process which lends itself to computerisation. Not only would information technology enable reminders to be generated automatically, it would also provide management information on bottlenecks in the system and on the performance of the LEA in completing the process to time.

CHECKLIST FOR ACTION – MANAGING THE PROCESS OF ISSUING STATEMENTS

Action by LEAs	Action by schools	Action by both	Already in place?	Action required?
Backlog of cases is monitored				
Time taken for each stage of the process is monitored				
Administrative methods and staffing levels are reviewed				
Strategy for increasing administrative staff at peak times is devised				
	Head teachers vet referrals to ensure school responsibilities are fulfilled			
	Known cases are referred as soon as possible, especially Year 6 pupils			
		Validity of referrals is agreed with educational psychologist		
Targets are set for officers involved				
Target times are agreed with district health authority and social services				
Performance in achievement of target times is monitored				
	Parents are encouraged to contribute to the assessment			
System to follow-up parents who do not contribute to assessments is implemented				
Liaison with social services department is undertaken, particularly concerning residential placements on social grounds				
Use of information technology in the administration of the process is investigated				

Source: Audit Commission/HMI.

5. Delegating Resources to Schools

55. Most LEAs fund extra adult help for pupils with special needs. This may be in the form of support for individual pupils in class, for sessions when pupils are withdrawn from class to receive intensive tuition, or for preparing specialist materials. LEAs have been cautious about the delegation of resources for the support of pupils with special needs. The experience of those LEAs which have delegated such resources to schools is that delegation confers many advantages. For example, if the school directly employs the extra support teacher, travel time is eliminated or reduced, co-ordination with the classroom teacher is facilitated and the support can be scheduled more flexibly to fit the pupil's timetable. Some LEAs fear that schools would not use special needs resources for their intended purpose. The fear arises because LEAs have not generally set up systems to ensure that schools are called to account for work with pupils with special needs. Advice on setting up systems to call schools to account is given in the next section of this handbook.

(i) RESOURCES FOR PUPILS WITH SPECIAL NEEDS BUT WITHOUT STATEMENTS

56. To delegate funds to schools, LEAs must apply a formula, as required by the 1988 Education Reform Act. LEAs have experienced difficulty in finding a factor within the formula which accurately reflects the incidence of pupils with special needs in ordinary schools. In the absence of primary indicators of the incidence of special needs, some LEAs have used proxy indicators, such as the number of pupils receiving free school meals. But there are ways of identifying the actual incidence of pupils with special needs in schools. LEAs should consider establishing systems to assess the number of pupils with special needs in LEA-maintained and grant-maintained schools as the basis on which to allocate funds through the formula which LEAs are responsible for devising under the 1988 Education Reform Act.

57. The approach adopted by Clwyd LEA (see Box C), although originally designed to improve the identification of pupils with special needs for educational reasons, also provides a primary measure of the incidence of special needs and illustrates one method of identifying how much extra funding each school should receive in recognition of the number of pupils with special needs on roll. Kent LEA adopted a different strategy to achieve the same end (Box F, overleaf).

58. Kent's approach is based on an assessment of the amount of extra help over and above ordinarily available provision which those needs imply. Clwyd's approach is based on an assessment of the degree to which those pupils are failing to make progress. Both are valid and illustrate that the delegation of funds can be based on primary rather than proxy indicators of special needs. The DFE have indicated[1] that any such approach which is based to a significant

---

1   *Source: correspondence with the Audit Commission/HMI study team.*

37

THE BASIS FOR THE ALLOCATION OF SPECIAL NEEDS FUNDS TO LEA-MAINTAINED AND GRANT-MAINTAINED ORDINARY SCHOOLS IN KENT
Schools in Kent undertake an annual audit of the number of their pupils with special needs

Since 1989 Kent LEA has undertaken an annual audit of the number of children with special educational needs. Class teachers complete a profile of the amount of support, additional to what is normally provided by the school, required by pupils with special needs. This is to enable the LEA to determine whether and how much additional money to allocate to schools.

Different schools may assess the extra help required by pupils with similar levels of need from different baselines, depending on the degree to which each school sees it as part of its own responsibility to provide for pupils with special needs in the normal course of its work. This could lead to schools with different levels of need receiving the same level of funding. To counteract this, the LEA undertakes a training programme, insists that teachers specify what extra input they themselves are making, and then moderates schools' returns.

This moderation takes place at two levels: clusters of schools analyse a sample of each others' returns and the LEA assesses a sample which is representative of each cluster. The sample examined includes both a random sample and returns from selected schools which appear to be failing to administer the process properly.

The LEA has two levels of need in its audit which trigger additional funds. They reflect bands into which pupils with special needs are grouped, based on the level of additional help which they require (Table 1). Pupils are registered at level one when their presence results in relatively minor modifications to the provision which schools make for all pupils. Schools are expected to make some of this provision from their basic funding. For example, pupils are registered at level one if they require:

— **'** differentiation of schemes of work, tasks, materials, assessment and recording

— modification of material/recording

— greater than normal parental liaison

— release time for staff to attend case conferences **'**

or a number of other enhancements to the provision which is generally available for all pupils.

Table 1

KENT LEA'S FORMULA FOR SPECIAL EDUCATIONAL NEEDS FUNDS FOR LEA-MAINTAINED AND GRANT-MAINTAINED SCHOOLS
Allocations for 1992/93

Level of need	% of maintained pupil population	Amount allocated via formula	
		Primary	Secondary (Yrs 7 to 11 only)
Level 1	11.3%	£245	£140
Level 2	11.6%	£245	£340

Schools with more than 50% of their pupils on level 1 or above receive an additional £225 for each pupil in excess of 50%

Source: Kent LEA.

> To be registered at level two, the child's needs must lead to more significant enhancements being made by the school to supplement the education which is provided for all pupils. Such enhancements include:
>
> — **'** additional focused support in planning and implementing specific objectives within the National Curriculum
>
> — aids shared with a small group of other pupils (1 – 4)
>
> — extended periods of observation. **'**
>
> In 1993/94, the LEA will be introducing a total of six levels of funding. Registration at level three will be reserved for pupils whose special needs require the school to make major changes to be able to provide appropriately for the pupil. The other levels of funding will apply primarily to children in special units or special schools, although occasionally they will be used for pupils with more severe difficulties who are placed in ordinary classes.

degree on subjective judgement will have to satisfy the Secretary of State for Education that there are sufficient moderation procedures for ensuring that the allocation of funding will be equitable.

59. LEAs' funding formulae will reflect the actual incidence of special needs in schools only if people who are in a position to assess the needs of individual children are involved. The key to success in Kent has been training teachers to conduct the audit and then instituting systems which enhance consistency. The moderation of schools' assessments by LEAs gives such schemes credibility, and the involvement of schools themselves in the process of moderation helps them to accept that it is a fair system.

60. Primary indicators of special needs provide more than a means of delegating resources equitably to schools. They also provide a more accurate picture of the proportion of the total school population which is identified as having special needs than is possible in LEAs which use proxy indicators. In Clwyd, 16% of the pupil population are entered on the register, and in Kent the figure is 23%. Kent LEA is concerned that this figure may be too high and is intending to work with schools to focus resources on a smaller proportion of the pupil population.

61. It is important that resources are allocated on the basis of the current level of need in each school, and reviews of the incidence of pupils with special needs should be conducted annually. Teachers should assess whether pupils' special needs remain above the threshold determined by the LEA for the school to receive extra funds. Schools with a greater number of pupils with special needs have a higher workload, but they stand to gain more funding than schools with few pupils with special needs. The cost is also higher in the first year of operation than in subsequent years, because schools have to identify all pupils with special needs in the first year, whereas in subsequent years they have only to update the audit, and also because they accumulate experience.

62. Under Kent's system, a school with 100 pupils registered under the audit would require approximately eight teacher-days for the audit in the first year and four per year thereafter. The cost to the LEA itself is £150,000 annually in training, printing and in paying for one day's teaching time for each school to cover teachers' attendance on the training course. No additional

LEA staff were appointed to administer the system, as it is considered that the audit improves schools' identification of pupils with special needs – a task already considered part of the inspectors' workload. Kent is one of the largest LEAs in the country, and smaller LEAs could expect significantly lower costs, particularly as such approaches will replace, in part at least, their current systems of resource allocation.

63. Clwyd's register and Kent's audit have educational benefits. They raise the awareness of ordinary school teachers of children's special needs and the process of updating highlights the need to re-assess the impact of classroom strategies undertaken to meet pupils' special needs.

CHECKLIST FOR ACTION – DELEGATING RESOURCES TO SCHOOLS FOR PUPILS WITH SPECIAL NEEDS WITHOUT STATEMENTS

Action by LEAs	Action by schools	Action by both	Already in place?	Action required?
System to establish the actual incidence of pupils with special needs in ordinary schools is established				
Levels of need which trigger registration are defined				
		Implementation plan is designed		
	Pupils with special needs are identified and registered			
		Schools' returns are moderated to ensure consistency with the defined levels of need		
Trend in proportion of school population registered is reviewed				
		The system is updated annually		
The allocation of funds for each level of need is set annually				

Source: Audit Commission/HMI.

(ii) RESOURCES FOR PUPILS WITH STATEMENTS

64. *Getting in on the Act* proposed changes to the format of statements to focus on the progress of pupils with special needs and facilitate delegation of funds so that schools could determine how to meet those objectives. However, there is much that LEAs and schools can do now while such changes are being considered. The delegation of funds for pupils with statements is likely to constitute a major variation in an LEA's scheme for local management of schools. Therefore there are several steps which LEAs must take, including consulting with schools and seeking approval from the Secretary of State for Education or for Wales, prior to setting up such a scheme (Exhibit 8).

Exhibit 8
DELEGATING FUNDS FOR PUPILS WITH STATEMENTS
There are several steps which LEAs should take in sequence

65. The essence of delegation is that schools should manage their own resources and determine how best to make the provision specified in statements. There are safeguards for ensuring that provision is made for pupils with statements once funds have been delegated. These include LEAs attending pupils' statutory annual reviews, amending statements to reflect changes in circumstances and ultimately the ability of the LEA to deliver the additional provision itself. Further, the DFE and Welsh Office[1] have stated that schemes of local management of schools should include an obligation on governors to deliver the provision specified in pupils' statements when resources for those pupils are delegated to the school.

---

1   *Circular 7/91 in England and 38/91 in Wales.*

66. To match resources to the needs of the pupil as closely as possible, the LEA should set up a funding formula which is flexible enough to cope with pupils with a wide variety of needs and for schools which are equipped to provide for these pupils to varying degrees.

67. Some LEAs have set up formulae through which pupils' needs are categorised into a few broad bands and schools funded accordingly. Pupils' needs may not fit neatly into such categories. This does not usually cause a problem in delegating funds to schools where such pupils have broadly similar needs and the school is funded for a group of pupils, for example in a special unit, which is large enough to result in over-funding of some pupils being counterbalanced by under-funding of others. In this case, using broad bands of funding can be appropriate. If LEAs adopt a number of bands of funding for places in special schools under local management of special schools, they could apply the same bands of funding to equivalent special units in ordinary schools. This would provide a consistent system of funding across both sectors. LEAs should, however, allow for the possibility that some pupils may have quite exceptional needs which fall outside the LEA's bands of funding. LEAs should hold some contingency funds centrally to provide 'top-up' funds in such rare cases.

68. Where pupils with statements are placed individually or in small numbers in ordinary schools, schemes with broad bands of funding may result in over- or under- funding because the combination of the wide variation in pupils' needs and in schools' facilities makes it unlikely that funding can be determined accurately using only a few broad categories. LEAs should consider adopting a different approach for delegation of funds in respect of these pupils with statements.

69. Leeds LEA is now in its third year of delegating resources to schools for pupils with statements (Box G, overleaf). Leeds' original use of a few coarse bands meant that it often over-funded pupils. It has now changed its system to cost pupils' and schools' requirements more accurately. The LEA assesses pupils' needs and then makes an individual allocation of funds, the amount of which is determined by reference to a set of principles which the LEA is developing. The LEA tries to be accurate to the nearest £500, but there are practical limits to the accuracy with which funds can be targeted. Unless a pupil's sole requirement is for specific items of equipment, precise prediction of the teaching methods required for a pupil is not possible because schools may need to change their approach several times. But it is possible to be more accurate than the nearest £1,000 or £2,000. As the levels of funding are so high, and can continue for several years, it is cost-effective for LEAs to spend time achieving accurate allocation of resources.

70. Leeds LEA is now in the second year of its modified scheme and reports that parents find it easier to accept decisions on the allocation of funds because an attempt has been made to allocate a sum of money to the school which reflects the child's and the school's circumstances. Leeds uses this approach for the delegation of funds for all pupils with statements. LEAs could also consider implementing this type of scheme only for pupils placed singly or in small numbers in ordinary schools, and use bands of funding for special units and special schools.

71. LEAs cannot make arbitrary decisions on the level of funding required. To conform with the Education Reform Act, they must publish the principles, rules or methods by which they determine the allocation of funds to schools for pupils with statements. This should include details of the factors which will be taken into account when deciding whether schools should be funded differently for pupils with similar needs.

DELEGATING FUNDS FOR PUPILS WITH STATEMENTS IN LEEDS
Leeds' formula for the funding of schools allows it to determine the amount of funds to be delegated to schools for pupils with statements more accurately than most LEAs' formulae

Leeds LEA delegates funds for pupils with statements of special needs in cases where schools have the skill to meet pupils' needs. The funding for pupils with statements for most types of need is delegated, but not funding for some pupils, such as those with sensory impairments. Leeds does not think that its ordinary schools have the expertise to enable the responsibility for the day-to-day management of those pupils' education to be delegated, although this situation is currently under review.

To delegate funds for pupils with special needs, LEAs must devise a formula and use consistent criteria to determine the allocation of resources to schools. In the first year of operating a scheme for the delegation of these funds, Leeds set up three bands of funding, with a fourth band for pupils in special units in ordinary schools. The bands were defined by reference to the level of extra help which was required by pupils with special needs (Table 2).

Table 2

PREVIOUS CATEGORIES OF FUNDING FOR PUPILS WITH SPECIAL NEEDS IN LEEDS LEA

Band	Description	Annual allocation (1990/91)
A	Small group work with a small amount of teacher or non-teaching assistant time	£880
B	Half-time support from a non-teaching assistant or the equivalent in teacher time	£4,460
C	Full-time non-teaching assistant or a half-time teacher	£8,800

Source: Leeds LEA.

In practice, Leeds found that pupils' individual requirements did not fit readily with these wide bands. Therefore the LEA had to decide whether to fund a pupil at a level higher or lower than that indicated by an assessment of the child's needs.

In the second year of operation it set up a new system. Each child was individually assessed, and the provision required was costed. The LEA then allocated a number of funding units to the school, with each unit having a value of £500.

Leeds is refining its statement of the criteria on which it bases its decisions. These criteria include factors which relate to the capability of schools to provide for a pupil with special needs. Where a school has already developed skills and materials in providing for pupils with a particular type of special needs, subsequent pupils after the first may attract a lesser level of funding. For example, the LEA placed one child with Down's Syndrome in an ordinary school and funded the school to create special teaching aids to help the pupil study the same subjects as his peers. When the school was asked to take another pupil with Down's Syndrome and with a similar level of need, the school, parent and LEA agreed that a lower level of funding was appropriate, as the school had already prepared teaching aids for the first pupil which could be used for the second.

Leeds delegates resources not only from the LEA to schools, but also within the LEA itself. The officers responsible for writing statements in the different geographic divisions of the LEA have responsibility for managing a share of the budget for pupils with statements, and for reallocating resources when they are no longer required.

Schools are advised that staff whose employment is funded by a statement should not be employed on a permanent basis unless the LEA offers a guarantee of long-term funding. If schools do so and the LEA subsequently amends the statement to reduce the level of provision, schools have to pay any additional costs which are incurred. The flexibility in reallocating resources which this approach allows, together with the delegation of the rôle of monitoring to a level where the individual officer can know when circumstances change or the pupil leaves the school, means that Leeds is able to claw back and re-use funds far more quickly than most LEAs.

72. LEAs should evaluate regularly whether the resources delegated to schools continue to be required or whether adjustments are necessary. Such control can be achieved in practice only by delegating the responsibility for the budget within the LEA to officers whose span of managerial responsibility is small enough to allow for frequent contact with schools, and who are in a position to know when there may be an opportunity to reallocate resources. Schools which take on staff whose employment is dependent on the funds received via the statement must ensure that the terms of employment of those staff allow for the possibility of changes in, or cessation of, the funding.

CHECKLIST FOR ACTION – DELEGATING RESOURCES TO SCHOOLS FOR PUPILS WITH STATEMENTS

Action by LEAs	Action by schools	Action by both	Already in place?	Action required?
Decision is taken to delegate funds for pupils with statements				
LEA decides if funds for pupils with certain types of need will be exempt				
Safeguards are in place (paragraph 65)				
Outline of scheme is drawn up indicating factors relating to pupils and schools to be taken into account when allocating funds				
		Consultation with schools undertaken		
		Scheme of local management obliges governors to deliver the provision specified in statements		
Proposals are submitted to Secretary of State if they constitute a major variation in the scheme of local management				
Rules, methods and principles of the scheme are published				
The value of funding units is set annually				
	Terms of employment of staff reflect the possibility that funding may be changed			
The allocation of funds for pupils with statements is reviewed annually and statements amended				

Source: Audit Commission/HMI.

6. The Accountability of Schools and LEA Support Teams

(i) MONITORING SCHOOLS' PERFORMANCE WITH PUPILS WITH SPECIAL NEEDS

73. LEAs should monitor the achievements which schools make with pupils with special needs. Whilst inspection will provide some information on the performance of schools, more regular and summary information on performance and on the impact of LEA policies is needed. Schools need feedback on how well they are succeeding in helping pupils with special needs in order to review their teaching strategies.

74. Many schools and LEAs are reluctant to use objective measures of schools' performance in the field of special educational needs because they believe that such indicators give only a partial impression of schools' work in special needs and are therefore misleading. Such reluctance is based on a misconception of the purpose of performance indicators. Performance indicators should trigger investigation of the reasons why particular schools achieve well and others may be failing, and lead to appropriate action. LEAs can investigate only a small number of schools at any one time, and therefore it is helpful to have a global picture of schools' performance to enable the LEA to determine where to investigate and which schools to help.

75. There are several possible performance indicators – they can relate to academic performance, as described in this section, or they can relate to other areas of schools' performance in special needs, such as the degree to which pupils with special needs are integrated into ordinary classes in a school. Many schools and LEAs already gather information on pupils' reading ability and numeracy which can be used for the purposes of monitoring schools' performance in special needs. The individual scores of pupils can be accumulated school by school, and the LEA can then compare the initial scores of pupils of lower ability with their re-test scores three or four years later. The average progress of pupils of lower ability in each school can be compared, giving an indication of schools' performance in this area.

76. Reading ability is only one area of a child's education and therefore information about it relates to only part of schools' work with pupils with special needs. That is not a reason for failing to make use of this type of objective data. It is a reason for placing such information in the context of other information which LEAs may have about schools' work – from inspections, for example.

77. A straightforward comparison of schools' progress in this area does not take into account other factors, such as the socio-economic status of schools' pupils, or the level of ability of all pupils in the schools' intake. Other methods of comparing schools which take account of these factors can be used. Solihull LEA co-operated with the study team to investigate how its data on pupils' reading ability could be used in this way (Box H).

COMPARING SCHOOLS' PERFORMANCE WITH PUPILS OF LOWER ABILITY

Comparisons between schools can take account of pupils' neighbourhoods and of the level of ability of all pupils on intake

Solihull, like many LEAs, has for some years gathered information from schools about pupils' ability in reading. Reading tests are administered to all pupils in their third and final years in primary school and to some pupils in their first year in secondary school. The results indicate to teachers which pupils may need extra help in reading and give the LEA a picture as to whether standards are improving. They can also be used as a performance indicator. The study team and LEA undertook an exercise to illustrate how such data can be used to assess schools' performance in improving the progress in reading made by the pupils of the lowest ability in a sample of the LEA's primary schools.

The LEA identified nine pairs of primary schools in which both schools in each pair served the same area. In the view of the LEA, the pupils in both schools in each pair were of similar socio-economic status. The reading ability of all pupils in their third year in both primary schools in each pair was compared, as was the reading ability of the lowest scoring 20% of pupils in both schools. Comparisons between schools' performance were made only where these were similar in both schools. The LEA and study team could therefore be confident that they were comparing schools on an equitable basis. This is important because the performance of pupils may be affected by their level of ability early on in their school careers, the level of ability of other children in the school, and their economic circumstances. As the average ability of pupils enrolling at primary schools varies from year to year, performance data was gathered for a period of several years to give an accurate picture.

The study team and LEA then measured the progress made by the lowest achieving 20% of pupils in their next four years in school.

The results indicate which school in a pair consistently achieves a better performance (see exhibit below). Comparisons can also be made between larger numbers of schools, but since this will include schools serving different areas, the comparison does not take into account the different socio-economic backgrounds of the pupils, although it does take into account the different levels of ability of the pupils early on in their school careers. The results indicate even greater differences in performance between schools with lower achieving pupils of similar levels of ability early on in their school careers (see exhibit on facing page).

This information gave the LEA a snapshot of the performance of its ordinary schools with pupils who were significantly behind their peers in a fundamental skill. On its own it did not tell either the schools themselves or the LEA how far these differences in performance were due to factors which were within the control of the schools and LEA.

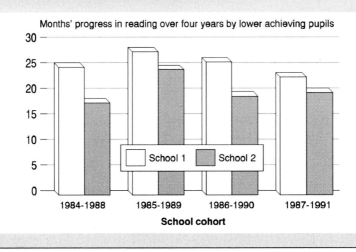

Months' progress in reading over four years by lower achieving pupils

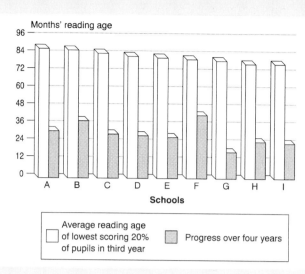

Therefore, an inspection visit focusing on reading was arranged for Schools 1 and 2 in the exhibit on the facing page.

The characteristics depressing School 2's performance were:

— the classroom practice of teachers in the school was not monitored by the head teacher

— no records of pupils with special needs were passed from teacher to teacher, so each teacher had to assess afresh which pupils had special needs and had no knowledge of which teaching methods had previously succeeded or failed with individual pupils

— there were low expectations of what pupils could achieve in all subjects

— no individual teacher in the school had overall responsibility for reading

— use of the library by pupils was not supervised by a teacher and on occasions pupils chose books which they could not read

— school-to-home reading initiatives had not been pursued

— two pupils who could not read at 10 years of age had not received statements from the LEA

— the staff at the school had greater experience and therefore tended to be more expensive than at the neighbouring school, leaving little room in the budget for the school to employ non-teaching assistants to help in class.

The strategies which lifted School 1's performance were:

— the school used the deputy head teacher to provide extra support in reading at Key Stage 1 of the National Curriculum

— the school had set up a system of recording the progress of pupils with special needs through which 'intervention sheets' for each pupil, indicating which teaching methods had worked well or not, were passed among the teachers

— the head teacher used the data from reading tests to monitor the school's performance from year to year

— there was a greater level of parental involvement

— pupils had a silent reading session every day.

78. The approach adopted in the case example is to use the results of reading tests to indicate the value which schools have added to pupils' education. The same approach should be used with the results from National Curriculum assessments as these are progressively implemented. This will highlight the performance of schools with pupils with special needs in all areas of the curriculum.

79. Parents may be interested to know how well all pupils in a school perform – irrespective of their ability on entering the school – in order to make informed decisions when stating their preference for a school, but on its own this information may not be adequate. To make a fully informed decision, parents need to know the school's performance with pupils with a similar level of ability to their own child. Schools and LEAs should present information on schools' performance in adding value to the education of pupils based on a comparison of their levels of ability on entering and leaving the school.

80. Information on performance is as valuable to schools as it is to parents and LEAs. Head teachers can use the results of reading and other tests to assess the impact of different teaching strategies and to help determine priorities for the use of extra resources. Indicators also prompt classroom teachers to review the amount of time spent on, for example, reading in classes which are under-performing in this area.

81. There are other means in addition to the use of performance indicators which LEAs should use to call schools to account for work with pupils with special needs. Attendance by LEAs at annual reviews of children with statements of special need is also a part of monitoring schools' work. *Getting in on the Act* recommended that educational psychologists should attend the annual review of every pupil with a statement at least every two years. The report indicated that in most cases this could be achieved by redeploying existing resources. To fulfil the rôle of champions of children with special needs, LEAs must objectively assess whether the provision made by a school for a pupil with a statement, and the school placement itself, remain appropriate.

82. Annual reviews should focus on pupils' achievements in relation to their potential. They should give a clear overview of the progress made by the pupil, including the use of objective measures. Objective measures are available for children with even the greatest disability, where progress may be assessed in terms of an improved skill in basic aspects of independent living, such as dressing or feeding. These supplement the subjective assessments made by teachers and help ensure that parents, the LEA and the school itself have a full picture of the child to form a basis on which to judge whether current provision is appropriate or whether the child could achieve more if resources were used in a different manner.

83. LEAs could enhance accountability by offering parents a rôle in completing the annual review form, in addition to inviting them to attend the annual review, the latter being a practice which is already common. Lincolnshire LEA, for example, sends the annual review form to parents and only considers the process to be complete once it has received comments back. LEAs should consider including questions for parents such as whether they find the present placement acceptable and on their level of satisfaction with their child's schooling.

CHECKLIST FOR ACTION – MONITORING SCHOOLS' PERFORMANCE WITH PUPILS WITH SPECIAL NEEDS

Action by LEAs	Action by schools	Action by both	Already in place?	Action required?
		Data on academic performance of pupils is gathered		
	Progress made over time by pupils of lower ability is analysed			
The value added by different schools to the education of pupils of lower ability is compared				
	Corrective action is undertaken if comparisons reveal that this is necessary			
Under-performing schools are investigated				
		Annual reviews of pupils with statements focus on pupils' progress against their potential		
Annual reviews are attended at least biennially				
		Appropriateness of current provision and placement questioned during the annual review		
Annual review form redesigned to encourage parents to express views				

Source: Audit Commission/HMI.

(ii) MONITORING THE PERFORMANCE OF LEA SPECIAL NEEDS SUPPORT TEAMS

84. As well as monitoring the effectiveness of schools with pupils with special needs, LEAs should monitor the effectiveness of their teams of special needs support teachers. LEAs retain such teams partly to ensure that schools do not divert pupil support to other purposes – an issue which has been addressed previously (see Section 5(i)) – and partly because LEAs claim that such teams are better qualified than the support teachers which ordinary schools could deploy. Most head teachers visited by the Audit Commission/HMI study team do not accept that LEA services for pupils with general learning difficulties provide a better quality of support than they could provide themselves.

85. As with schools' work with pupils with special needs, objective criteria should be used to indicate the performance of support teams. These indicators will flag to managers when further investigation is required. None of the LEAs studied had themselves carried out a review of the effectiveness of support teams. However, the District Audit Service has undertaken some work in this area in conjunction with an LEA and it provides a useful example of how such performance monitoring can be carried out (Box I). The indicator used in this case example – progress in literacy skills made by the pupils supported by the service – covers a relatively narrow range of achievement, but it is relevant to the work of a service for which the development of literacy skills is a priority.

86. The success of support teams should not always be measured only by the amount of progress made by pupils with special needs whom they support. Some schools may have only limited experience of providing for pupils with special needs and may require both direct support for specific pupils and general guidance. An evaluation of the effectiveness of such teams should take into account any rôle in increasing schools' capabilities, as this could be an important factor in encouraging ordinary schools to provide for pupils with special needs when those schools might otherwise have neither the confidence nor the ability to do so. However, LEAs should assess whether this advice could be more appropriately provided by advisory teachers or educational psychologists.

87. Performance indicators should not be used as the sole basis on which teachers' work is judged. They should serve to highlight situations where the service is not having the desired effect and to trigger further investigation. Objective information of this nature is important because the credibility of the whole team depends on each school's perception of the effectiveness of the individual support teacher allocated to them. The support team in the case example in Box I was able to provide some objective evidence of its effectiveness and to identify situations where it was not succeeding so that it could take action to maintain its credibility. This will be particularly important for support teams in LEAs where funds will be delegated to schools for them to buy services from the LEA support team or from other organisations, or to provide support for pupils with special needs with staff directly employed by the school.

88. With such information, LEAs are in a position to compare the performance of pupils helped by the support team with the performance of pupils of a similar level of ability helped by the schools themselves and thus to decide whether the losses in efficiency involved in using peripatetic teachers are outweighed by any greater effectiveness.

Box I
MONITORING THE PERFORMANCE OF LEA SPECIAL NEEDS SUPPORT TEAMS
Performance monitoring can be applied to LEA special needs support teams to highlight areas where management attention is required

The District Audit Service conducted a review of the value for money offered by the special needs support team in an LEA which it was auditing. In collaboration with LEA officers, it assessed the impact of the support service on the progress made by pupils receiving the service's help.

As the elected members of the LEA had resolved that the major priority for the service should be to help pupils make progress in literacy, it was reasonable to use the results of a test designed to measure pupils' progress in literacy (the Salford Sentence Test) as one indicator of the effectiveness of the support service. The District Audit Service analysed the progress made by all pupils who had been supported by the special needs support service in a sample of schools. It assessed the progress made during the average period of support (18 months). It was thus able to review the effectiveness of the service in each school.

This analysis indicated that the service was largely successful in helping pupils to gain ground in their literacy skills at a faster rate than that which would be due to their increase in age. However, there were significant differences between schools in the effectiveness of the service. The analysis showed that in one school the ability of a significant proportion of pupils declined relative to their chronological age when the support service was involved.

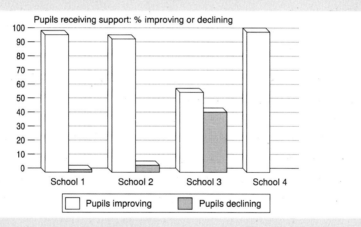

A more detailed investigation revealed that the problem in the school was one of poor co-ordination between the support teacher and the school. At the school's suggestion, the support teacher was carrying out work which did not focus on the development of literacy skills, and yet the pupils were being withdrawn from classes where they would otherwise have been focusing on literacy skills. This explains why they fell further behind in this area. Until this exercise was carried out, the LEA and school had been unaware of the impact of their approach.

Since the LEA did not have the resources to monitor the progress of every pupil receiving extra help from the service, the LEA and schools required management information of this kind to enable them to assess the effectiveness of the service overall and to help decide where more detailed investigation was required.

The District Audit Service also questioned a sample of head teachers as to whether the support service had been helpful in enabling schools to develop their own skills in providing for pupils with special needs. Although a majority of them found the service helpful, they also found this aspect of the team's work to be indistinguishable from similar help provided by advisers and educational psychologists.

CHECKLIST FOR ACTION – MONITORING THE PERFORMANCE OF LEA SPECIAL NEEDS SUPPORT TEAMS

Action by LEAs	Action by schools	Action by both	Already in place?	Action required?
Indicators of the performance of special needs support teams are identified				
		The performance of support teams with a sample of, or all, pupils supported is evaluated		
		The performance of the special needs support team is compared with the performance of schools with similar pupils		
The decision not to delegate resources to schools for this service is reviewed in the light of the above				
If the support team also provides guidance to schools, an evaluation is made as to whether this duplicates advice provided by others, e.g. advisory teachers				

Source: Audit Commission/HMI.

(iii) THE ACCOUNTABILITY OF SCHOOLS FOR THE RESOURCES WHICH THEY RECEIVE FOR PUPILS WITH SPECIAL NEEDS

89. Local management empowers schools to manage their own resources. Schools should be made accountable for the progress which they enable pupils with special needs to make. They should also be called to account for the way in which they have actually spent those resources. This does not undermine schools' discretion to manage their own finances, nor does it imply that LEAs can tell schools how to spend resources delegated to them in respect of pupils with special needs without statements. It enhances schools' accountability and informs LEAs of the impact of their schemes for formula funding schools.

90. Where a school appears to be under-achieving with pupils with special needs, it is important that LEA and independent inspection teams and auditors assess whether part of the problem is that schools have not been applying the right level of resources or have not been managing those resources in the most effective manner. Even when schools are performing well with pupils with special needs, the LEA should decide whether the amount of funds delegated to schools for this purpose remains appropriate. This applies to funds delegated to schools in respect of pupils with special needs both with and without statements. One LEA undertook an exercise to assess how a sample of schools had used resources delegated to them to educate pupils with statements (Box J). A similar approach can be used to assess the provision made for pupils with special needs but without statements.

91. An analysis of how schools have used resources delegated to them in respect of pupils with special needs involves more than counting the number of extra hours of teaching support provided by the school. The school may have required class teachers in all a pupil's subjects to prepare special materials, rather than allocating an individual adult to support a pupil, or, for example, it may have decided that the provision of a computer system more effectively meets a pupil's needs. These are valid approaches and all consume resources which would not be accounted for simply by totalling the hours of additional adult support provided.

92. It is not appropriate, when costing the provision made by the school for pupils in ordinary classes, simply to divide the teacher time by the number of pupils in the class to get an average amount of teacher time spent on the pupils with statements. For example, one of the schools reduced class sizes by some 30% when pupils with statements for moderate learning difficulties were placed in them. Although pupils without statements may also have benefited from the smaller size of the class, the school assessed that it could integrate these pupils fully – an aim which the 1981 Education Act obliges LEAs to pursue – only if it reduced the class size. The cost to be taken into account was therefore the cost to the school of reducing the class size, not the cost of the average amount of teacher time given to pupils with statements. However, had the school used this money to reduce all class sizes, even when pupils with statements were not placed in them, this would have been an inappropriate use of those funds.

93. Some LEAs use a few broad bands of funding as the basis for funding special units in ordinary schools or for schools with special facilities or for what are described as 'resourced schools'. It is inherent in this approach that some pupils with lesser needs will be funded to the same degree as other pupils with greater needs. It is not appropriate to criticise a school which may spend less on one pupil than the amount which is delegated in respect of that pupil if the

CALLING SCHOOLS TO ACCOUNT FOR THEIR USE OF SPECIAL NEEDS RESOURCES
Schools should be asked to account for the way in which they have spent special needs funds

The inspectorate of one LEA undertook a review of the provision made by six ordinary schools which had received delegated resources to provide for pupils with statements of special educational needs placed in special units in the schools. In all six schools, the pupils spent only part of their time in the unit, the rest of the time being spent in ordinary classes. This review involved both a qualitative analysis of the provision made for pupils and an assessment of the amount of extra help given. This case study focuses on the latter, as the issue of qualitative inspections is the subject of a further case study.

The two inspectors conducting the review asked the schools to provide individual timetables for every pupil with a statement, indicating:

— the amount of time spent by the pupil in ordinary classes

— the amount of extra support provided for the pupil when taught in an ordinary class

— the number of other pupils with whom such support was shared

— whether the support was provided by a teacher or ancillary worker

— the amount of time spent in withdrawal groups

— the number of other pupils in withdrawal groups.

They used this information to assess and cost the amount of extra help provided by the schools for each pupil. Where teaching took place in small groups, they estimated each pupil's share of the teacher's time.

The inspectors obtained details of the amount of funds delegated to the school in respect of each pupil and read the pupils' statements. The inspectors calculated that there was a gap between the amount of money allocated by the LEA in respect of each group of pupils and the amount spent on directly supporting them. In some cases the whole class size had been reduced to facilitate the integration of pupils with learning difficulties who would otherwise have had to spend more time in special units. This involved extra cost and accounted for some of the shortfall.

However, in some of the schools, although the provision made for the pupils was appropriate, there was still a gap between the funds allocated by the LEA and the provision made by the school. In some schools, this arose because there were temporarily empty places in the units. These places were still funded, but at a lower level than occupied places. The LEA reports that these schools demonstrated that funding for the empty places was being appropriately used temporarily for other pupils with special needs pending the places being filled. Where the surplus was not accounted for, the LEA's scheme of formula funding allocated greater amounts of money than were required to provide appropriately for those pupils, indicating that the LEA should review its scheme of formula funding.

The inspectors found that the schools developed expertise and materials on behalf of pupils with statements which were also useful in the schools' work with other pupils with special needs. The inspectors did not make any deduction for this from the calculation of the cost of what the school was providing for the pupils with statements, as this was seen as a legitimate and economic use of educational resources.

school is spending more than the delegated amount on other pupils with statements, so long as the school is providing appropriately for all of them.

94. Where there is still a shortfall between what the school provides and the amount of the funding for pupils with statements, even allowing for the factors described above, the LEA should assess whether it is funding these pupils to a greater degree than is necessary, or whether schools should be pressed to provide still further help from within the resources already delegated on the grounds that with that extra help the pupils would be capable of still greater progress.

95. Information on the different types of help provided by schools can also reveal the degree to which pupils with special needs are integrated into ordinary classes. It is common that data which is gathered as part of the process of costing also reveals useful objective information on patterns of educational practice.

CHECKLIST FOR ACTION – THE ACCOUNTABILITY OF SCHOOLS FOR THE RESOURCES WHICH THEY RECEIVE FOR PUPILS WITH SPECIAL NEEDS

Action by LEAs	Action by schools	Action by both	Already in place?	Action required?
A sample of schools in which to evaluate use of special needs resources is selected				
	Timetables of a sample of pupils with special needs and an overview of the school's special needs strategies are provided			
Amount of extra help provided for pupils with special needs is assessed				
		Any apparent shortfall is discussed to reveal other inputs		
Pupils with special needs are observed and their work examined or recent inspection reports reviewed to assess if provision is appropriate				
		If special needs funds are not fully or effectively used to achieve the intended objectives and provision is not appropriate, an action plan for more effective use of resources is drawn up		
If funds are not fully used to achieve the intended objectives and provision is appropriate, levels of funding in scheme of local management are reviewed				

Source: Audit Commission/HMI.

(iv) EVALUATION OF CLASSROOM PROVISION

96. The direct observation of children in the classroom is a vital part of the overall assessment of schools' work, although the rôle of the inspector is broader than evaluating classroom practice alone. Inspectors should also use objective measures to assess the performance of schools in helping pupils with special needs to fulfil their potential and should assess the quality of provision in the whole school. However, an assessment of schools' achievements in making progress with pupils with special needs in the classroom will provide essential feedback for them on the impact of their special needs strategies.

97. When undertaking classroom observations, LEA special needs inspectors have tended to concentrate their attention on methods of teaching. But effectiveness is more accurately measured by reference to the progress which individual children make in relation to their potential. While observation of the educational process may highlight why sufficient progress is or is not being made once the rate of progress has been established, on its own it does not tell whether progress is being made. Inspectors who evaluate classroom practice in relation to pupils with special needs should focus on the impact of the lesson on individual pupils with special needs. They should supplement their direct observations of pupils with information from school records to gain a broader picture of the pupils' potential and progress.

98. This approach gives the inspector a firm basis on which to challenge the school where practice in the classroom is not effective. It also means that a lesson will not be faulted when the teacher has used an approach which, whilst not generally considered effective with pupils with special needs, is effective in particular circumstances. For example, it is not generally considered helpful to pupils with learning difficulties if the whole class undertakes the same task with no differentiation to take account of individual pupils' needs. However, if one pupil's special needs arise from an emotional and behavioural disturbance, such a structured approach with the pupil following the same instructions as the rest of the class might be what that pupil requires to enable him or her to make some progress in the lesson. The Audit Commission/HMI study team drew up a number of indicators of the impact of classroom practice on pupils with special needs in schools in the study LEAs. These were then used by the study team inspector as the basis for his lesson observations in schools in the study LEAs (Box K, overleaf).

99. Some school managers undertake this type of evaluation of classroom practice themselves to monitor the effectiveness of particular forms of organisation. This is an example which other schools should follow. *Getting in on the Act* highlighted an urgent need for schools to evaluate the use of support staff. The lack of planning of the time of support staff diminishes their impact in improving the quality of learning for pupils with special needs. Direct observation by senior members of the school's staff will help reveal if the use of extra adult help in the classroom is being planned and whether some of the time currently spent by support staff alongside pupils should be redirected into planning the lessons with the teacher. This issue is considered in part two of this handbook.

In each lesson, a pupil with special needs, with or without a statement, was selected to be the focus of the inspector's observations. The detail of the lesson was then observed from the viewpoint of that pupil. The inspector also made a short assessment of the response of the whole class to the lesson. The principal measure which the inspector used was an assessment of the target pupils' learning – or consolidation of existing skills – during the lesson. This involved observation of the pupils, examination of their written work, and a discussion with them to reveal how much they had understood and their perception of the purpose of the lesson. In addition, the inspector assessed the impact on the pupils of a range of other contributory factors.

Class:

No. on register: Age:

Target pupil this lesson: No. present:

Detail of staffing:

Description of lesson:

Effectiveness of deployment of support staff:

Suitability of the learning environment to target pupil's needs:

Match of resources to target pupil's needs:

Match of lesson content to target pupil's capability:

Proportion of target pupil's time 'on task':

Target pupil's independence in learning:

(Key measure) Pupil's actual learning or useful consolidation of existing skills or knowledge in the lesson:

Grading for whole lesson:

(Key measure) Grading for quality of target pupil's learning:

CHECKLIST FOR ACTION – EVALUATING CLASSROOM PROVISION

Action by inspection teams	Action by schools	Already in place?	Action required?
Observation of individual pupils with special needs is scheduled into school inspections			
Records of pupils to be observed are examined for background information on their progress and potential			
Schedule of pupils' responses to be observed during lessons is drawn up			
	School managers observe individual pupils in classroom to assess impact on them of teaching strategies and use of support staff		

Source: Audit Commission/HMI.

7. Controlling Special School Costs

100. As staffing costs account for 80% of special school budgets, there is significant motivation for LEAs to adjust the staffing levels of special schools. With a pupil:adult ratio of 3.5:1 on average, and 2:1 in special schools for pupils with severe learning difficulties, the movement of even a small number of pupils offers the opportunity to adjust staffing levels. With special school rolls falling, this means that LEAs have the opportunity to release resources from special schools and reallocate them to the support of pupils with special needs in ordinary schools.

101. As LEAs introduce schemes for local management of special schools, the number and type of places and pupils which they decide to fund will be the major determinant of staffing levels. DES Circular 11/90 and Welsh Office Circular 58/90 will be helpful to LEAs in assessing the level of funding which will be required by special schools to employ sufficient staff to provide for the needs of the pupils they have on roll. However, the two Circulars should not be used on their own to set staffing levels. They should be supplemented by the LEA's own assessment of the staffing needs of their special schools, as these will depend on the facilities in each LEA's special schools. In any case, a proportion of all LEAs' special schools will have pupils with needs which do not fit easily with the categories of need outlined in the Circulars and therefore will require separate consideration.

102. Formula funding of special schools, which will be introduced by LEAs by April 1994 at the latest, will help to ensure that special schools are funded on a consistent basis. It will not automatically result in special school staffing levels being adjusted in response to changes in the pupil population, as LEAs may draw up schemes which fund special schools on the basis of the number of places which have historically been provided and not largely on the number of pupils in them. Thus, excess staffing could continue to be funded if the LEA does not adjust the number of places which it funds. Once formula funding is introduced, instead of LEAs adjusting staffing levels directly, adjustments will arise as a result of changes in the funds allocated to schools through the formula.

103. Nottinghamshire LEA's experience throws light on how an LEA can take the first steps in tackling the issue of releasing surplus resources from special schools whilst retaining an element of flexibility for special schools to manage their staff (Box L, overleaf). Nottinghamshire is a large LEA, with 12 special schools for pupils with moderate learning difficulties. Smaller LEAs have fewer special schools, but they also can learn from this experience. The issue is not the size of the LEA – it is the amount of spare capacity in each school which determines how much adjustment can be made. Nottinghamshire was able to release amounts of teacher time ranging from 8.9 teaching posts from one school with 129 pupils on roll to no posts from a school with 100 pupils on roll (Exhibit 9, overleaf). Many smaller LEAs have special schools of a similar size and they also should review staffing levels and adjust them where appropriate. All LEAs should evaluate

Box L
REALLOCATING SPECIAL SCHOOL STAFF IN LINE WITH CHANGES IN THE PUPIL POPULATION
Nottinghamshire was able to release surplus teaching staff from special schools to support pupils with special needs in ordinary schools

Nottinghamshire LEA introduced a strategy to increase the capability of ordinary schools to provide for pupils with special needs, particularly pupils with moderate learning difficulties. The LEA expected that, in consequence, the population of its special schools for pupils with moderate learning difficulties would decline. It had planned a full review of special needs provision, including a review of special school staffing. However, the number of pupils in special schools for pupils with moderate learning difficulties declined more quickly and more sharply than anticipated, creating an unexpected level of over-staffing – at the same time as there was a heavy demand for resources from ordinary schools which were now providing for the pupils who would have attended the special schools.

The LEA decided that it was not appropriate to wait until the full review as this would cause a delay in action to get better value for money. However, it also did not want to pre-empt decisions which might be made on the basis of long-term plans arising from that review.

The principal educational psychologist was charged with implementing an interim solution to this problem. The LEA used DES Circular 11/90 as one guideline for staffing levels in its special schools for pupils with moderate learning difficulties, supplementing it with the educational psychology service's assessment of the needs of pupils in those special schools. This suggested that an average pupil:teacher ratio of 10:1 was appropriate. The LEA allowed each school an additional 'flexibility factor' of 0.5 teacher per school. A number of schools with pupils with quite exceptional needs were considered individually by the educational psychology service and LEA.

The LEA conducted the interim review openly and, as was expected, met opposition from the head teachers of some special schools. In response, the LEA increased the 'flexibility factor' to one teacher per special school for pupils of primary age with moderate learning difficulties and 1.5 teachers per special school for those of secondary age. In principle, this was to take account of mid-year pupil admissions. But the impact of mid-year admissions is counterbalanced to some degree by mid-year leavers. In practice, this was a reasonable concession by the LEA to give special schools time to adjust to this new situation.

Having identified the size of the surplus, the LEA's next task was to release it for supporting pupils with special needs in ordinary schools. As an interim measure, the LEA guaranteed that no special school would lose any staff permanently until the full review had been carried out. Each head teacher was then given a clear statement of the amount of teaching time to be released.

The LEA did not prescribe how the special schools were to release the teacher time. Each special school head teacher could decide the proportion of any individual teacher's time which was to be released. This assisted them in planning to deliver the National Curriculum, as they could decide when teachers with expertise in a particular subject in the National Curriculum would be available to teach in the special school and when they would be released to provide support for pupils with special needs in ordinary schools.

The LEA redirected over £1 million of surplus staffing from special schools into the support of pupils with special needs in ordinary schools.

Exhibit 9
RELEASING TEACHING RESOURCES FROM SPECIAL SCHOOLS IN NOTTINGHAMSHIRE
The number of teachers who can be released has little to do with the size of the school

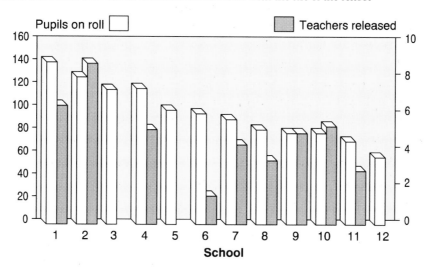

Source: Audit Commission/HMI fieldwork in Nottinghamshire LEA.

annually the number of staff or, after the introduction of local management of special schools, the number of places required in special schools.

104. The principle of releasing staffing resources should apply not only to situations where there are long-term changes in the pupil population. The pupil:adult ratio in special schools is so low that the movement of even a few pupils may release significant amounts of staff time during the course of a year. It may not be appropriate to adjust staffing levels during the course of the year, particularly if it is anticipated that spare places in the school will be filled in the near future. Special schools and LEAs should consider using the temporary surplus for activities outside the school altogether – in particular for the support of pupils with special needs in nearby ordinary or other special schools.

105. If special schools can respond flexibly in this manner, there is potentially a new rôle for them. *Getting in on the Act* recommended that where pupils with statements require very specialist help, such as the support of a teacher qualified to work with pupils with a hearing impairment, ordinary schools should have a choice of supplier of the support specified in the statement. LEAs could approve a range of suppliers of such specialist services – including special schools. In order to ensure that special schools do not give subsidies to ordinary schools by inadvertently charging for such services at an uneconomic level, which could consume resources which should be used for the special school's own pupils, the amount to be recouped by special schools for the provision of such services should be set by LEAs. These amounts could then be offset against the special school's budget by the LEA. In this manner, greater value can be gained from staffing resources which cannot be permanently released from special schools and special schools can be given the opportunity to develop a new rôle.

106. In some cases, the fall in pupil numbers has been, or will be, such that it threatens the viability of the school. The LEA must take a number of factors into account when deciding

whether to retain such special schools. An LEA may quite reasonably wish to keep such special schools open if to close them would involve pupils who would continue to require a special school place in travelling excessive distances. Cost is only one factor here. Such circumstances may mean that the LEA should undertake a more wide-ranging rationalisation of special schools and this is the subject of the next section.

CHECKLIST FOR ACTION – CONTROLLING SPECIAL SCHOOL COSTS

Action by LEA	Action by special schools	Action by both	Already in place?	Action required?
Format for assessment of staffing needs of special schools is drawn up				
Provision is made for special schools with pupils with exceptional needs				
		Assessment of staffing needs is conducted and results communicated to head teachers		
Number of teaching and non-teaching assistant hours, if any, to be released from each school is identified				
	Surplus staff time is released			
		Decision is made on whether staff can be reallocated immediately or whether they should temporarily remain in special schools, with the surplus time identified spent in ordinary schools		
Where immediate reallocation is not possible, timescale for permanent reallocation of staff is set				
		Use of special schools as approved suppliers of specialist services to ordinary schools is considered		
Scheme for the recoupment of costs of services provided by special to ordinary schools is established				

Source: Audit Commission/HMI.

8. Rationalising Special School Provision

107. The case for rationalising the provision of special school places, in addition to adjusting staffing levels, is growing. Special schools are now required to deliver the full National Curriculum, but small special schools, especially those providing for secondary age pupils, find it difficult to deliver the broad range of subjects required with a small establishment of teachers. The reduction in the number of pupils means that special school premises may not be used to their full potential. In addition, some LEAs have found that the degree of specialisation within the special school sector (severe learning difficulties, moderate learning difficulties, emotional and behavioural disturbance, etc) means that special schools serve very wide catchment areas. This involves pupils in travelling long distances, which is undesirable for the pupils themselves and an unproductive use of resources. In the White Paper, the Government stated an intention to give the Secretaries of State for Education and for Wales powers to require LEAs to bring forward proposals to rationalise special schools, and to make their own proposals for an LEA's special schools if they judge it necessary.

108. LEAs are keenly aware of the emotive nature of proposals to rationalise special schools. Elected members are rightly cautious in making changes which have an impact on vulnerable members of society. However, caution must not lead to inaction when resources fail to meet needs as effectively as they could if deployed in another manner. This recommendation to LEAs to rationalise special schools and at the same time attempt to avoid alienating parents, governors, the voluntary bodies working in this area and special school staff is made in the full knowledge of how difficult a task it is. It will require careful consideration by elected members and a most painstaking process of consultation with the parents of pupils in special schools and the voluntary bodies which promote their interests, as parental preference must be one of the guiding principles of such rationalisation. The experience of Leeds LEA illustrates some of these points and provides a useful case study of how some of the problems can be tackled (Box M, overleaf).

109. The key to success is exhaustive consultation with parents, governors, voluntary bodies and school staff. It is advisable for the LEA to meet these groups separately as this avoids their respective interests becoming confused. The number of schools involved is small enough for it to be practicable for the LEA to give detailed consideration to every special school and its pupils. The amounts of money involved in the education of each pupil are large enough to make this case-by-case consideration cost-effective. This process should take place in the context of an absolute determination on the part of the LEA to address radically the problems which are facing special schools. If there is any doubt about the LEA's resolve, such consultation will focus on whether positive action should be taken at all rather than on how it can further the interests of children with special needs in special and ordinary schools.

RATIONALISING SPECIAL SCHOOL PROVISION IN LEEDS
A comprehensive programme of consultation, taking account of parents' views, and a firm resolve to make the best use of special needs resources were the keys to success

Between 1978 and 1987, the special school population in Leeds had fallen by 40% from 2250 to 1370 pupils, creating almost 900 surplus places. Some special schools had as few as 10 pupils on roll, which represented a significant under-use of premises and involved high costs per pupil of running the premises. A programme of enhancement of provision for pupils with special needs in ordinary schools had been undertaken between 1986 and 1988 and this had accelerated the reduction in special school admissions. A number of special schools were also experiencing serious difficulty in teaching a full range of subjects to pupils. A review reporting to the Education Committee in 1988 contained proposals to rationalise special school provision.

The scope of the initiative was purposely limited. It addressed only special schools for pupils with moderate or severe learning difficulties, with the other special schools being considered at a later date. It was not part of a further drive to place a greater proportion of pupils with special needs in ordinary schools and did not include any review of the competence of staff, with a view to pruning less competent staff.

The reorganisation was made the responsibility of a single senior officer, although two additional staff were seconded from schools. One of them held responsibility for staffing issues and liaising with parents. It was particularly helpful that this person was a special school head teacher as this provided some reassurance that he had an understanding of the practical issues involved in managing a special school. The other member of staff had oversight of all matters concerning buildings and other resources in the amalgamation process.

The LEA stated that all special schools in the categories affected (21 out of the LEA's total of 24 special schools) were to be regarded as closing, and that the LEA would then re-open a reduced set of new special schools. Although some of the re-opened schools might be in the same premises and under the same names as before, none could assume that it would provide for the same type of pupils as before.

The process of consultation involved a group of officers including a member of the LEA advisory team and of the LEA policy team attending separate meetings with the governing body, the staff and the parents for each special school affected by the review. Each of these groups in every school was offered the opportunity of up to three meetings with officers. With 21 special schools involved and up to three meetings for each of three groups, the LEA's consultation programme involved a commitment to 189 meetings with groups affected by the plans.

The basis on which the LEA held discussions was that there was an absolute necessity for change, which was not open to question. The purpose of the meetings was to consult on the best means of making changes in the LEA's special school provision which would secure the maximum advantage for pupils and their parents.

The LEA was subject to considerable lobbying from parents, voluntary bodies, staff and the community at large. For example, a petition to keep open a school for pupils with severe learning difficulties was signed by 6,000 local people and presented to the council.

Suggestions and objections were logged at each meeting, hence the LEA was able to highlight changes to its plans which had arisen specifically as a result of the consultation period.

The feedback from these meetings indicated to the LEA that Leeds required some special schools for pupils with both severe and moderate learning difficulties in the same school, as the continued integration into ordinary schools of the more able pupils with moderate learning difficulties meant that the previous differences between pupils in the different types of special school were now not so pronounced. The LEA decided that it required some schools which catered for pupils from 5 to 19 years and other schools which provided only for primary aged pupils or secondary aged pupils. Where these plans involved a change of school for a pupil, parents were offered the opportunity for their children to change to schools different from those proposed by the LEA.

Governors were given training seminars on the process for the redeployment of school staff so that a consistent interpretation of the LEA plan was put forward.

As part of the proposals, the LEA committed itself to refurbishing some of the premises which were to be retained, and gave an assurance to parents and staff that it would replicate particular features of closed premises, such as a hydrotherapy pool in one school, as far as could be achieved within the LEA's capital spending limits. Given the surplus of premises which had been one of the factors prompting the review, the LEA was able to choose the best premises, from the point of view of location and facilities, from those available.

The reorganisation resulted in the closure of 21 schools in August 1991 and the re-opening of 11 new schools in September 1991, giving the LEA a total of 14 special schools as three had been unaffected by the rationalisation (see maps below). It was estimated that the number of qualified teachers could have been reduced from 175 to 110, but a decision was taken to enhance staffing in special schools, not least in recognition of the wide age range of pupils in some schools, so that the final total of qualified teachers was 153. Non-teaching assistants were reduced in number from 125 to 106. The LEA made provision for a surplus of 25% of places, as it was feared at that time that the more competitive environment in which ordinary schools were operating, with pressure on them to improve examination results, could lead to an increase in the number of pupils attending special schools if ordinary schools did not give enough attention to pupils with special needs who might be perceived as contributing less than other pupils to schools' examination results.

Before rationalisation

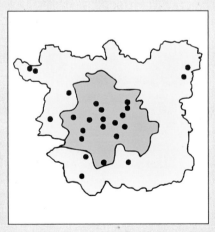

After rationalisation

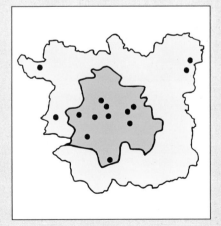

● Special school   ▢ City centre

This increase did not materialise, and the LEA now faces the challenge of addressing the remaining surplus of places, a task which it believes it can complete without changing the number of special schools which it maintains.

Although releasing a relative surplus of resources from special schools was only one of several factors prompting the rationalisation, the LEA released resources worth £1 million in the first year alone from classroom staffing and premises running costs, with further savings in auxiliary and administrative staff in schools yet to be calculated. In addition there is the prospect of income from the sale of disused sites. The LEA has stated its intention to spend these funds on pupils with special needs in other areas of the education system.

110. A willingness to take parents' views fully into account is another prerequisite for success. The LEA should produce evidence of how its proposals have changed in the light of consultation with parents. This means keeping parents informed as the process of consultation continues and offering them the widest possible choice of schools for their children.

111. Quick action to appoint the head teachers of newly formed special schools is required so that the parents of pupils who have to move as part of the rationalisation can meet the head teacher and have access to a professional with whom they can discuss concerns about their child's education.

112. The involvement of elected members of the LEA at each stage is essential. In some LEAs, plans to rationalise special school provision have been drawn up, causing anxiety to parents and involving considerable amounts of officer time, only to be rejected by elected members. The view of elected members should be sought at each stage of the consultation to ensure that the plans being evolved are consistent with their policies for the LEA and to ensure that members are fully aware of the reaction from parents and the community.

113. Leeds LEA had a commitment to retaining special school provision as one of the choices open to parents of pupils with statements. The LEA believes that this was a major reason for its success in gaining parents' support. Even though the long-term policy of the LEA is that pupils with special needs – particularly those whose learning difficulties are moderate – should be educated in ordinary schools, the LEA is flexible. Its declared aim is that parents who state a preference for a special school education for their child should have their wishes fulfilled. This does not mean that an LEA has to retain special schools where these are required for only a handful of pupils, as the practice of using spare capacity in neighbouring LEAs is already commonplace. Indeed, in some cases, special schools in another LEA will be closer to a child's home than their own LEA's special schools.

114. This example illustrates what can be achieved by careful planning and painstaking consultation within the context of a clear commitment to get better use from existing resources to the benefit of both the current special school population and of pupils with special needs in ordinary schools.

CHECKLIST FOR ACTION – RATIONALISING SPECIAL SCHOOLS

Action by LEAs	Action by special schools	Action by both	Already in place?	Action required?
Review of special school provision highlights need for rationalisation				
Elected members commit themselves to rationalising special schools. The need for change is presented as non-negotiable				
LEA agrees to provide special school places for parents who state a preference for them				
		Head teachers are consulted/seconded to the LEA		
Parents are consulted				
Voluntary bodies are consulted				
		Governors and staff are consulted		
Changes made as a result of consultation are publicised				
Elected members commit the LEA to implementation				
		Governors are briefed on implementation programme		
	Head teachers of special schools to which any pupils are moved are accessible to parents early in the process			
		The number and type of places in special schools are rationalised		

Source: Audit Commission/HMI.

Part Two:
Improving the Quality of Learning for Pupils with Special Needs

Additional issues for schools and teachers

Preface to Part Two

115. The new relationship between LEAs and schools, in which schools are the 'contractor' in a client/contractor relationship gives schools a significant rôle. School governors should set and monitor the school special needs policy. Schools will be responsible for identifying pupils with special needs and for working with the LEA to increase their capability in this area. Increased delegation of funds for pupils with special needs with and without statements will ensure that schools have the maximum available resources for their work. They will also have to demonstrate achievements in the eyes of parents if they are to attract pupils with special needs and their attendant resources.

116. These changes bring more responsibility, more delegation of resources – and more accountability. As LEAs and schools act on the recommendations in this handbook, schools' performance with pupils with special needs will be more rigorously monitored than before. This handbook does not provide an exhaustive list of all the ways in which schools can improve practice in the classroom. It describes good practice in three areas which were highlighted in *Getting in on the Act*. Schools also need to address the issues described in part one of this handbook.

9. Improving the Quality of Lessons for Pupils with Special Needs

117. The presence in a class of pupils with special needs challenges teachers' ability to organise lessons to ensure that all pupils make progress. There are several strategies which teachers can adopt to help pupils with learning difficulties who are working within larger groups of pupils. Although the strategies outlined in this and the following sections are already widely understood by teachers in ordinary and special schools, they are only infrequently put into practice.

118. Teachers can differentiate the methods by which they present a lesson to meet the individual pupils' needs (Box N). This involves some planning prior to the lesson to enable the teacher or classroom assistant to select the materials or prepare the approach which will enable the pupils to follow the lesson. Differentiation in the presentation of lessons can be applied to groups of pupils as well as to individuals. Some class teachers plan for the class to cover the same subject but at two levels of ability (Box O, overleaf). There is a need for this type of differentiation whether there is extra adult help in the class or not. Without it, the rôle of the extra adult is reduced to coaxing pupils through a lesson which they are barely capable of comprehending and explaining the task to the child rather than working on it with the child. This does not mean preparing a different lesson for these pupils – teachers do not usually have the time to do this – but fine-tuning the lesson which they have already planned.

Box N
DIFFERENTIATING THE METHOD OF TEACHING FOR PUPILS WITH SPECIAL NEEDS
Differentiating the method of teaching often helps pupils with special needs follow the same lesson as the rest of the class

> In Ravenscroft secondary school in Barnet a Year 7 pupil with specific difficulties in reading was working like the other pupils in the class on a booklet from a commercial maths scheme. This scheme allowed for pupils to work at their own level of ability. The head of the school's centre for pupils with specific learning difficulties had tape-recorded the content of the booklet, and the pupil used the tape-recording successfully to augment his own reading of the text. This meant that he was not prevented from addressing the mathematics because he could not easily read the instructions in the book and also that he incidentally practised his reading skills.

119. To be able to differentiate materials according to pupils' needs, teachers must know those needs in some detail, and to do this, teachers should have a system of assessing and recording pupils' needs and the progress which they make. The best classroom recording systems are easy

DIFFERENTIATING LESSONS FOR GROUPS OF PUPILS
Providing for more than one level of ability in a class is a practical strategy for teachers

> A Year 5 class in Mere Oaks special school in Wigan had been working on a topic about the local coal industry. The lesson was bringing to a conclusion the work on the formation of coal. The most able pupils were given large pieces of blank paper on which to compose sets of pictures illustrating the sequence of events in coal formation. Those needing more guidance were given teacher-made outlines to be coloured and annotated. There were, in addition, posters and books around the room which pupils could use according to their level of ability and there were actual samples of coal and fossil ferns which they could use to help them complete the task. The prepared materials differentiated between the two levels of ability of the pupils, and the supporting materials were such that all pupils could use them to differing degrees.

to complete, and are compatible with or part of other assessment systems which teachers maintain. They should identify pupils' strengths and weaknesses and measure their progress. It is particularly useful to record which teaching strategies accelerated pupils' progress (Exhibit 10). Some schools have a standard system for recording the progress of pupils with special needs in all classes. This saves teachers 're-inventing the wheel' and ensures that teachers who are new to the pupil can see which approaches worked and which did not. The use of information from assessment and recording systems is the key to improving the match of classroom work to pupils' particular needs.

Exhibit 10
ASSESSING AND RECORDING THE PROGRESS MADE BY PUPILS WITH SPECIAL NEEDS
The best systems are simple and form part of existing assessment and recording systems

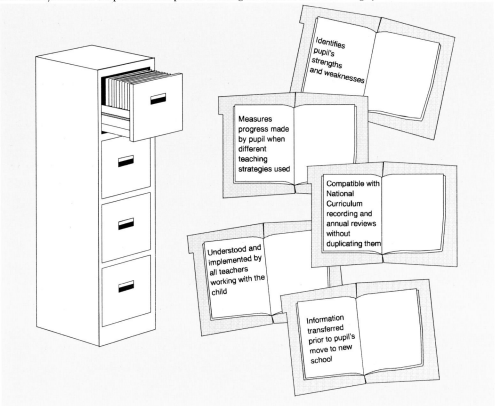

120. Another effective strategy is to have available resources which are particularly appropriate for pupils with special needs which they can use independently during lessons to help them achieve a task. Special dictionaries, reference books and information technology designed for pupils with special needs are all widely available. With some initial training, pupils can use these, promoting independence in learning as well as reducing their demands on the teacher (Box P). In the primary age range in ordinary and special schools, this approach is made easier because pupils spend a large proportion of their time in the same classroom, a régime which is quite different in secondary schools. Tutorial periods in secondary schools can be used to promote pupils' independence in learning, but the approach needs to be planned across subject departments, with materials appropriate to each subject available to pupils. Some secondary schools are encouraging the independent use of special materials by changing the function of rooms which used to be the base for remedial classes into 'drop-in' centres where pupils may go at their own behest for assistance or additional resources in several different subjects.

Box P
HELPING PUPILS WITH SPECIAL NEEDS TO HELP THEMSELVES
Providing some extra aids to learning to which pupils with special needs can turn at their own behest can develop their independence in learning

A class teacher in Lea Frances Olive Anderson primary school in Lincolnshire worked alone with a class of 28 pupils including one boy with moderate learning difficulties. This pupil was in a group working on posters on hygiene to illustrate points from a talk given by the school nurse the day before. At the start of the task, the pupil with special needs moved around the room collecting the resources he thought he might need. Available to him were a book on calligraphy, a simplified dictionary and a book on the topic which the teacher had taken out of the school library in case he should need it.

The library book gave the pupil the idea for the central character in his poster, the calligraphy book the rounded print style and the dictionary (with occasional help from his neighbour) gave assistance with spelling. The pupil with special needs did make more contact than other pupils with the teacher, but solely for reassurance.

The teacher felt it essential to develop his self-help skills in view of his special needs and his impending transfer to secondary school. To this end, she made an effort to keep some essential resources accessible for his use in spite of the cramped nature of the classroom.

121. Withdrawal lessons, where one or a few pupils are taken out of the main lesson for intensive coaching, are also a valid means of improving the quality of learning for pupils with special needs. However, they pose two problems: if pupils are consistently withdrawn from one subject to teach them another this will deny them the opportunity to learn the subject from which they are withdrawn; and they may interfere with the pupils' social experience in class. There is also a danger that withdrawal may involve only generalised practice of skills in literacy and numeracy without a focus on pupils' current difficulties in their work in the ordinary class. This approach should be used where there is a clear justification for spending the extra staff time on withdrawing pupils rather than supporting them in class or preparing special materials for them. The key to increasing the impact of withdrawal sessions lies in monitoring pupils' progress in one or two major areas of difficulty and ensuring that the sessions are co-ordinated with pupils' work in their ordinary classes.

CHECKLIST FOR ACTION – IMPROVING THE QUALITY OF LESSONS FOR PUPILS WITH SPECIAL NEEDS

Action by teachers	Action by schools	Action by both	Already in place?	Action required?
Teachers can describe target pupils' individual needs				
Materials and activities are differentiated				
		Resources for independent use by pupils with special needs are available		
		If pupils are withdrawn, it is for short periods of intensive work related to pupils' current classwork		
	There is a standard system for recording pupils' special needs and the success and failure of strategies to help those pupils make progress			

Source: Audit Commission/HMI.

10. Managing Extra Adults in the Classroom

122. Extra adults supporting pupils with special needs in the classroom are an expensive resource, the use of which should be prepared in advance if the cost is to be justified. Planning and communication are the crucial factors in using that additional support to best effect. For example, it is not uncommon for a supporting adult to sit through a lesson with virtually no useful rôle because the style of the lesson precludes working with individual pupils. Examples of this are class discussions and use of audio-visual resources. With a degree of planning, the supporting adult need not spend the whole time in the lesson (Box Q).

Box Q
PLANNING THE USE OF EXTRA ADULTS IN THE CLASSROOM (i)
Advance planning of extra adults' time can release them from lessons where they will be of limited use to undertake work which will have a greater impact

> A support teacher for a blind pupil in Byrchall High School in Wigan reviewed with the science teacher the unit of work for a Year 8 class on the human digestive system at the beginning of term. Work sheets for the lesson had been translated into Braille and diagrams simplified and photocopied on to special sheets which gave a tactile image. The support teacher stayed for five minutes at the beginning of the lesson, ensuring that the pupil knew her way around the worksheets and understood the slight differences between her materials and those of the rest of the class. Discussion with the science teacher as the class came in had suggested a means of presenting a particularly difficult task is such a way that the blind pupil could tackle it independently. The support teacher accordingly spent the first half of the lesson in his small workshop corner refining this material. He delivered it part way through the lesson, incidentally checking that the pupil and teacher were coping, then returned to the support base to make more materials for future lessons.

123. In contrast to the more typical pattern of in-class support which involves the adult sitting alongside the pupil, support through preparation and planning does not isolate the pupil socially from his or her peers. This way of working is particularly appropriate for the support of pupils with sensory impairment, but the principle is applicable to many forms of special need. Its successful application depends on an initial investment in forward planning to:

— agree when the supporter's presence is necessary and when not

— develop an initial set of differentiated materials which will confer increased independence upon the pupil, thus freeing more support time in future for preparation of more differentiated materials.

The outcome is a 'beneficial circle', in which professional time is used to modify resources which enable the pupil to exercise more independence, thus freeing further professional time. The alternative is for the pupil to be faced with unsuitable materials which need (or even defeat) adult mediation, or which reduce the adult to the rôle of telling the pupil the answers to fill in on a worksheet.

124. The supporting adult should be aware of the class teacher's objectives for a piece of work so that he or she can then focus on what the child is to master, and consider alternative means of reaching the same goal. While working alongside pupils is the principal rôle for supporting adults in ordinary schools, joint planning with the teacher can raise the quality of their work. Although this may take a small amount of time away from the direct support of pupils, the impact of that support will be increased significantly. At present, support staff often arrive in the classroom without preparation, which means that planning is limited to a few hurried moments at the start of the lesson. In special schools, non-teaching assistants tend to work consistently with particular teachers, and here their rôle is more readily established by informal consultation and by a knowledge of classroom routines. In the best examples of practice, non-teaching assistants in special schools contribute to other aspects of classroom management such as record keeping.

125. Teachers in both special and ordinary schools can be faced with a complex management task when they have to organise more than one additional adult in their class. Most lessons with more than one adult in support are very poorly organised in both special and ordinary schools. The establishment of a well planned but flexible network of adult rôles in the classroom is a particular challenge, and it demands an insight into the strengths of the individuals in the team (Box R).

PLANNING THE USE OF EXTRA ADULTS IN THE CLASSROOM (ii)
Where there is more than one extra adult in the classroom, advance planning enables the teacher to alter the pattern of support in response to changes in the pupil's needs without necessarily becoming directly involved

A class in St. Chad's Church of England primary school in Oldham with Year 3 pupils included a boy with learning difficulties and behavioural problems. He received part-time support from a classroom assistant and two short sessions of support weekly from a teacher based in a nearby special school. As the pupil's needs had changed, the classroom assistant's support had been switched from break and lunch times to morning lesson periods, with a consequent change in rôle from encouragement of socialisation to individual academic support. The teacher from the special school had access to specialised materials and equipment and had particular expertise in the planning of individual educational programmes. She took a lead in collating records of the pupil's progress and in planning modifications to activities prepared for the whole class, relieving the class teacher of much of this task.

In the lesson, the pupil had dictated some notes from reference books to the classroom assistant, and was experimenting with transcribing these on to a small electronic typewriter brought in during the lesson by the special school teacher. The classroom assistant was watching the process closely so that she could take the lead in overseeing the pupil's use of the machine in the absence of the specialist teacher, thus once again reducing the burden on the class teacher.

The planning behind this lesson involved:

— exploiting the strengths of the specialist teacher

— adjusting the timing of the classroom assistant's contribution to match the pupil's changing needs

— encouraging the specialist teacher to liaise directly with the classroom assistant in order to relieve the class teacher of the need to learn the workings of a new piece of technology in mid-lesson.

CHECKLIST FOR ACTION – MANAGING EXTRA ADULTS IN THE CLASSROOM

Action by teachers	Action by schools	Already in place?	Action required?
Teacher and supporting adult have agreed in which lessons there is a rôle for the latter			
Rôle of the supporting adult has been planned			
Teacher or supporting adult prepare special materials if necessary. To increase pupils' independence, consideration is given to preparing special lesson materials as well as providing side-by-side support			
	Time is allocated for communication between teacher and supporting adult		
	School managers observe impact of extra adults in classroom on pupils with special needs		

Source: Audit Commission/HMI.

11. Monitoring the Performance of Teachers with Pupils of Lower Ability

126. The increasing introduction of appraisal of teachers' performance offers an opportunity to apply at classroom level some of the principles of performance monitoring which apply at the level of the school and LEA. Teachers' performance with pupils with special needs should form part of the appraisal of their performance overall. This can help provide an incentive to teachers to make positive achievements in this area.

127. Many special and ordinary schools will be able to use assessments of individual pupils' progress through the National Curriculum as indicators of teachers' effectiveness with pupils with special needs. Where appropriate, objective measures of pupils' development of personal and social skills might supplement these indicators.

128. Where such an approach is not practical, for example in secondary schools which may have large numbers of pupils with learning difficulties taught by many different subject teachers, it is possible to identify and contrast the achievements of subject departments and individual teachers with pupils with special needs. The use of information technology in school administration offers the opportunity for such information to be gathered. School test and examination statistics provide one basis upon which the achievement of teachers with pupils of lower ability can be assessed (Box S, overleaf).

129. The academic achievement of pupils with special needs is only one indicator of teachers' performance. There are other important issues in providing for these pupils. For example, the 1981 Education Act encourages schools to educate pupils with special needs in ordinary classes and the performance of teachers and school departments in fulfilling this obligation should also be monitored. Similarly, communication with parents of pupils with special needs is an important part of teachers' work, particularly for pupils whose performance at school is sensitive to changes at home. However, the educational progress which pupils with special needs make must be an important indicator of schools' and teachers' success in providing for them.

130. There is a danger in this approach that if standards and expectations overall in a school are low, then the average performance of lower ability pupils will not reflect their potential and teachers will not be challenged to raise standards to the level which is achievable. For this reason it is important that schools and LEAs should adopt the recommended approaches to performance monitoring which involve external comparisons of performance between schools, as outlined previously, and between the school and national standards of performance such as GCSE results and results of National Curriculum assessments (Exhibit 11, overleaf).

Audenshaw High School in Tameside is a comprehensive, grant-maintained school in an urban area. For most subjects taught in the school, pupils are placed in teaching groups according to their ability in the subject. As well as producing a profile of the examination results of the whole school, the head teacher produces a profile of the examination results for each teaching group in every subject. The average result which those same pupils achieved in all the examinations which they took is also calculated by assigning GCSE grades A to G a numeric value. This overall average can be taken as a measure of the pupils' general academic ability. Their achievement in each subject area can then be compared against their overall achievement. For example, in the academic year 1990/91, pupils of lower ability in art achieved a better average score in that subject than they did in all subjects considered together. By contrast, pupils of lower ability in maths achieved significantly lower results in that subject than their average score for all subjects taken together. Pupils of lower ability fared significantly worse in history than in geography compared to their performance in all subjects considered together.

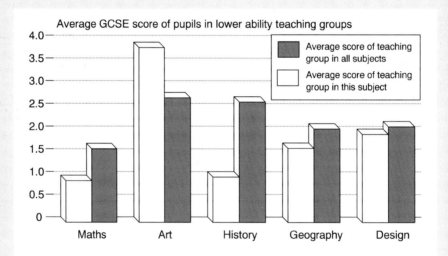

Heads of department and the head teacher at Audenshaw are able to use these results to highlight where teachers are under-achieving with lower ability pupils. As with all performance indicators, their purpose is to trigger further investigation. The level of achievement attained may be explained by factors which are not related to the teacher's performance – for example, the current teacher may only recently have assumed responsibility for the class. Any such background factors may, on investigation, prove to be relevant in explaining the achievements of the pupils in any given teaching group, but the starting point is objective information.

The academic performance of pupils is one of several factors which are taken into account during teacher appraisal in Audenshaw. Other factors are the teacher's contribution to the pastoral care of pupils and their contribution to extra-curricular activities in the school.

Exhibit 11

COMBINING INTERNAL AND EXTERNAL MEASURES OF PERFORMANCE

Comparisons of the performance of individual teachers should be supplemented with an external comparison of the school's performance

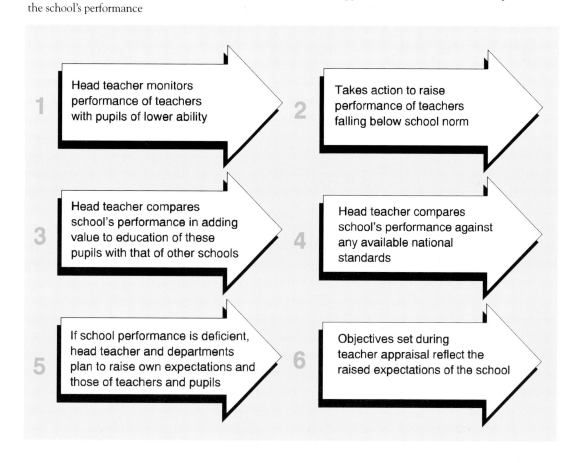

1 — Head teacher monitors performance of teachers with pupils of lower ability

2 — Takes action to raise performance of teachers falling below school norm

3 — Head teacher compares school's performance in adding value to education of these pupils with that of other schools

4 — Head teacher compares school's performance against any available national standards

5 — If school performance is deficient, head teacher and departments plan to raise own expectations and those of teachers and pupils

6 — Objectives set during teacher appraisal reflect the raised expectations of the school

CHECKLIST FOR ACTION – MONITORING THE PERFORMANCE OF TEACHERS WITH PUPILS OF LOWER ABILITY

Action by head teacher	Action by school management team	Already in place?	Action required?
An assessment of teachers' performance with pupils with special needs is included in appraisals			
	Objective indicators of progress made by teachers with pupils with special needs are included in appraisals		
Assessment of teachers' contribution in non-academic areas of special needs, e.g. work with parents, is included in appraisals			
	Use of comparisons of the progress made by pupils with special needs with different teachers is considered		
	Performance of school is compared with that of other similar schools, using objective data, e.g. LEA-wide tests or data on the results of National Curriculum assessments		
	School's performance is evaluated using national data on performance		
Review of school's expectations of teachers' and pupils' potential is conducted (Exhibit 11)			

Source: Audit Commission/HMI.

* * *

131. By implementing the proposed national guidelines on assessments and statements and by providing guidelines on the level of need in a child which should trigger extra help but not necessarily a formal statement, LEAs and schools can identify more consistently which pupils should be the target for extra resources and introduce greater clarity as to the respective responsibilities of schools and LEAs for those pupils. The introduction of systems at both LEA and school level to monitor the performance of schools for achievements they make with pupils with special needs, and for their use of resources delegated for special needs, will lead to significant improvements in the accountability of schools and LEAs in this area. The delegation of accurately targeted funds together with monitoring of performance which is designed to highlight positive achievements will help provide an incentive for schools to improve their level of achievement with pupils with special needs. The funds available to support those achievements can be increased by ensuring that special school provision is rationalised where necessary, and new rôles can be developed for special schools to provide an incentive for them to make the most effective use of their resources.

132. As LEAs and schools introduce greater separation of their respective rôles in the field of special needs, schools will have greater responsibility in this area, more autonomy, and more resources delegated to them – but more pressure to ensure that pupils with special needs achieve their potential. These actions are all important steps in improving the quality of provision for pupils with special needs.